Papua New Guinea is o... ...cal independence and this volume gives important insights into the way its inhabitants are dealing with the new political institutions that have impinged upon them in the last years of colonial rule. The title suggests both the scope of the book and its main theme: it is not a study of a single village but of a district; and recent developments have widened the political horizons of its inhabitants in interesting ways. Dr Morauta shows how the people of Madang interpret the institutions of political representation; and her book gives continuity to previous studies, for it also reports on the activities of the now famous cargo cult leader Yali and his supporters. Yali's cult has become virtually institutionalised and provides opportunities that compete with the administration's political structures for the individual's alignment.

The author is Lecturer in Anthropology and Sociology at the University of Papua New Guinea, Port Moresby.

BEYOND THE VILLAGE
Local Politics in Madang, Papua New Guinea

LONDON SCHOOL OF ECONOMICS
MONOGRAPHS ON SOCIAL ANTHROPOLOGY
No. 49

BEYOND THE VILLAGE

Local Politics in Madang,

Papua New Guinea

BY

LOUISE MORAUTA

UNIVERSITY OF LONDON
THE ATHLONE PRESS
NEW YORK: HUMANITIES PRESS INC.
1974

Published by
THE ATHLONE PRESS
UNIVERSITY OF LONDON
at 4 Gower Street London WC1
Distributed by Tiptree Book Services Ltd
Tiptree, Essex

USA and Canada
Humanities Press Inc

UK SBN 0 485 19549 6
USA SBN 391 00327 5

Printed in Great Britain by
T. & A. CONSTABLE LTD
EDINBURGH

For my father and mother in England
and my 'parents', Kaut Malok and
Elizabeth Nein, in Kauris

ACKNOWLEDGEMENTS

I am most grateful to the people of Madang for their cooperation, patience and kindness during my fieldwork. I owe a particular debt to Kaut Malok of Kauris, who is a good friend as well as a stimulating informant.

My 1968–9 fieldwork was financed by a number of different organizations, to all of which I am grateful. I was supported by the Social Science Research Council of Great Britain, the Emslie Horniman Scholarship Fund of the Royal Anthropological Institute, the Middlemore Educational Foundation and a Johnstone and Florence Stoney Studentship from the British Federation of University Women. Fieldwork on the 1972 national elections was generously financed by the University of Papua and New Guinea.

On the academic as well as personal side I should like to thank my doctoral supervisor at the London School of Economics, Anthony Forge, and Professor Peter Lawrence, now of the University of Sydney, for their help and encouragement. Professor Lawrence generously made his field notes and documentary materials available to me in Brisbane in 1968, visited me in Madang and collaborated in the 1972 election study. I have also benefited from discussion with Audrey Bolger, Sandra Bowdler, Dick Hueter, Alan Jarman, Peter McLaren, Nigel Oram, Anton Ploeg, Brian Ranson, Mary-Cath Regan, Roger Southern, Robert Waddell, Michael W. Young and members of seminars at the London School of Economics, the University of Papua and New Guinea and the University of Queensland. I am grateful to Mrs M. Ploeg of the U.P.N.G. Cartography Unit for her careful assistance with maps and diagrams, and to the U.P.N.G. photographic section for help with plates. None of the faults in this book are anyone's but my own. I am grateful to the editor of *Man* for permission to use in a different form material which appeared in that journal, September 1972, vol. 7, no. 3, pp. 430–47.

Finally my thanks go to my parents for their understanding during fieldwork and after I returned, and to my husband for his support while I was writing this book.

L. M.

CONTENTS

PLATES

between pages 92 and 93

FIGURES

TABLES

CASES

MAPS

Introduction

This book[1] is concerned with the social and political structure of an area in the hinterland of Madang, a town on the north-east coast of the mainland of New Guinea. The clan and village which were once key units in the political system have lost much of their political significance after nearly a century of contact with Europeans. In the past the village was the largest autonomous political unit. Today Madangs find themselves in the much wider political arena formed, for example, by church and local government organizations. New leadership roles are played within these new political structures.

The problem for investigation is the nature of today's political system and the place of the village in it. I ask whether these new institutions have created more than a nominal unity, and whether people really have begun to think and act politically in terms of a wider area than their own village. I argue that the answer to this question is different depending on whether we are looking at one or the other of two distinct types of political conflict. The first is what I have called 'pragmatic' conflict, in which villages are the base units in wider segmentary structures. The second is 'ideological' conflict, which divides villages internally and gives rise to alliances between groups in different villages. In the first case political identification beyond the village has not proceeded very far. In the second, which is associated with a differentiation of interests within the traditional political unit, a much greater sense of unity among people from different villages has appeared.

This subject is of more than academic interest. The kind of relationship which exists between villages is most important to the development of Papua New Guinea. Whatever form future governments take, they will all require some measure of integration between small traditional political units, in the case of Madang, villages. It is hoped that this study will contribute to an

---

[1] Based on my Ph.D. thesis (Morauta 1972a.)

understanding of the extent and nature of such integration as existed in one small area in 1968 and 1969.

THE AREA

The conventional anthropological study of a single village was inadequate as an approach to this problem, since it was essential to examine relations between villages. I was anxious not to pre-judge the issue by choosing villages according to some assumption about the basis of political grouping, for example according to common language or membership of a single ward in the local government council. Eventually I selected 17 villages which all lay in the immediate sub-coastal hinterland: Barahaim, Butelkud, Foran, Haidurem, Kamba, Kauris, Kesup, Korog, Mirkuk, Mis, Mukuru, Nobanob, Opi, Panim, Silabob, Urugan and Yahil.[1] Their location is shown in Map 1.[2]

These villages were selected for two main reasons. In the first place, they are all situated on the land which lies between the Gum and Biges Rivers and the coast. This area is said to have been the traditional territory of the Wagi people (Kamba speakers) among whom I lived. It has a clear geographical boundary. Seven coastal villages (Sek, Malamal, Riwo, Siar, Biliau, Kranket and Yabob), which fall within the same geographical limits, have been excluded because they are culturally and historically distinct from those inland. They speak Austronesian languages (Z'graggen 1969, pp. 189–192) and their legends tell of a more recent arrival in the area. Even traditionally they were short of land. They are fishermen, sea-traders and canoe-builders. Their traditional initiation ceremony included circumcision, which was not prac-tised by their non-Austronesian-speaking neighbours. To include these villages would have introduced an unnecessary complica-tion.

The second factor which influenced the choice of villages was my own location in Kauris. This was decided for me before I ever reached the field. When the Ambenob Local Government Council was told of my plans, the councillor from Kauris agreed to be my host. So it was that I went to his village. It proved to be an ideal

---

[1] Spelling as in Papua New Guinea 1968b, p. 83, except for the 'h' in Barahaim there which appears as 'm' I assume because of a printer's error.

[2] This and other maps are based roughly on Department of Lands, Surveys and Mines 1965 and 1971.

location politically, being almost equally divided between the two main factions in Madang. As can be seen from Map 1, Kauris is roughly in the centre of the area I chose to study, and this further recommended to me the selection of these particular villages. For brevity I regularly refer to this area as 'Madang'. For clarity, the town of that name will be referred to as 'Madang Town'. Madang Town itself was excluded from the study because it is politically distinct in many ways from the surrounding villages and would require a separate field study if any clear picture was to be obtained.

According to official records, in 1967 these 17 villages contained a population of 2,579 (see Table 1). This figure included some

Table 1. Population in the 17 villages

| Village | Years of census | | | | |
	1944/1945	1952	1957	1961	1967
Barahaim	121	N.A.	152	178	224
Butelkud	84	74	80	90	99
Foran	62	72	83	98	101
Haidurem	70	71	N.A.	90	103
Kamba	213	210	233	270	320
Kauris	103	N.A.	118	127	143
Kesup	N.A	N.A.	120	151	168
Korog	16?	N.A.	176	200	228
Mirkuk	103	N.A.	102	102	167
Mis	N.A.	N.A.	126	148	152
Mukuru	87	85	N.A.	85	98
Nobanob	238	258	291	336	393
Opi	40	60	40	36	44
Panim	61	76	83	96	114
Silabob	69	73	68	77	87
Urugan	64	N.A.	72	95	106
Yahil	N.A.	N.A.	55	74	32
Totals				2,253	2,579
Totals for villages for which all years available	767	823	878	1,003	1,158

Sources: Department of the Administrator, Division of District Administration (D.D.A.), Patrol Reports (various dates), Madang District and File 14-2-7, Census and Statistic, Madang District.

people who, in terms of my definition, would not be counted as village members. No pre-war records survived the Japanese invasion of 1942, but the post-war figures given in Table 1 suggest that the population is expanding, and this is confirmed by informants' impressions. In 1967 the administrative official conducting the census narrowed the definition of village membership considerably, with the result that Yahil lost more than 50 per cent of its population. Such vagaries make it quite unrealistic to calculate any precise rate of population increase. But a rough index of this is the proportion of people under 16 years of age: records show that this has risen from 33·2 per cent in 1944 to 45·6 per cent in 1967.

It should perhaps be emphasized that the 17 villages in no way form a corporate group. No single feature (apart from their location), either traditional or introduced by Europeans, distinguishes them collectively from their neighbours. They do not all speak the same language, or even languages of the same non-Austronesian family (Z'graggen 1969, pp. 40–7). Map 2 shows these linguistic groupings. Nor do they constitute a local government unit. Although they all belong to the Ambenob Local Government Council, they and several other villages make up six different wards (see Map 3). It follows that when I describe the Madang people I am not necessarily contrasting them with some other population. In fact much of what I say may apply to neighbouring villages too.

A DEFINITIONAL NOTE ON THE VILLAGE

The village is a key unit in this book. Its traditional composition will be described in Chapter 1 and its current role discussed in several later chapters. Here, however, I want to mention how I have arrived at a division of the population into the particular 17 village groups shown in Map 1. Some explanation is necessary, since the number coincides exactly neither with Administration records nor traditional history. I define a village as a cluster of interdependent clans. The Administration recognizes two units, Korog No. 1 and Korog No. 2 (Papua New Guinea 1968b, p. 83), whereas I treat Korog as a single village. Although it has a residential division into two parts, this is common elsewhere (e.g. in Barahaim), and the same clans appear in both settlements. Six of the groups which the Administration treats as units were traditionally two separate villages (Butelkud, Foran, Mirkuk, Opi, Urugan and Yahil). In each case one of the two is today considerably smaller than the other, and it may be that, even at the time of initial Administration contact, the two villages were for practical purposes combined because one was so small. I therefore take the name of the larger of each pair as that of a single combined village. A third kind of problem arises with Nobanob. Here it is difficult to say what the original clan cluster was, because in the 1860s (Inselmann 1944, pp. 13–14) the people migrated from further inland in several waves. These different waves of migration are recognized today in named groups of clans, but in terms of land ownership and residence the picture is more confused. I have therefore followed Administration practice and refer to Nobanob as one village.

One other element in my definition of the village can be mentioned here for the first, but by no means the only, time. Generally speaking the term will be used to refer collectively to those people who are members of the constituent land-owning clans. It excludes residents on village land who have no traditional rights of ownership there. The difference between the two is discussed in Chapter 3.

THE METHOD

It is apparent from Map 1 that the population studied is scattered over a wide area. Furthermore (and this is not obvious from the map) villages are commonly divided into several hamlets. Given the size and distribution of this population it is clear that the traditional anthropological technique of living and observing in one place was inappropriate for my study. The problem then was how to cover the whole area in adequate depth.

My answer was a combination of several techniques. For a depth study of the daily round of social life, the comings and goings of household and kinsmen, I concentrated on Kauris, living there from May 1968 to November 1969. Much of my detailed case material comes from Kauris. This does not seem to me to run counter to my aims. Certain topics, such as disputes and the relation between factions, cannot be treated cursorily. Either the anthropologist has a grasp of innumerable details and nuances, or he does not know what is happening. It was in Kauris that I got the necessary feeling for the *minutiae* of village life. It can also

B

be argued in favour of this method that what is true of Kauris is true to a certain extent of the other 16 villages. Despite linguistic and administrative fragmentation the area studied displays considerable cultural and social homogeneity, since the Austronesian-speaking villages were deliberately excluded. Other aspects of the study showed that family life, relations between kinsmen, traditional leadership, clan structure and subsistence agriculture – in fact those elements of traditional life which survive today – are largely common to all 17 villages. Differences in access to cash, roads and schools, and varying allegiances to Christianity and cargo cult have arisen since the arrival of Europeans. These do indeed vary from one village to the next. But such variations are considered in detail, and in relation to them no attempt is made to generalize from the experience of Kauris.

However, data clearly had to be obtained from all the villages. The problem was how to collect it in such a way that the conclusions could reasonably be applied to the whole area. I approached this in various ways. By doing in the other villages what I was already doing in Kauris, namely interviewing prominent men or those who proved particularly valuable as informants, I built up qualitative data on such subjects as pre-contact society and current views on leadership. I was careful to discuss the same topic in several different villages, to gauge consistency or its absence for the area as a whole. In addition to these more general enquiries I systematically asked certain questions in every village (Survey IV) and every clan (Survey III),[1] even when particularly gifted or cooperative informants were not available. Such systematic enquiries were made on subjects where it had become obvious that there was variation between villages (for example in their participation in cargo cults – Survey IV) or between individuals within them (on such questions as the origin of their wives and who supported Yali's cargo cult – Survey III). These latter questions were asked of senior members from every clan and yielded a very limited amount of information on all adult male village members.

So far I have discussed data obtained from a few cooperative individuals, largely involving their own experiences and opinions, and a very small amount collected second-hand about all adult males. But there was also a need to contact in some way at first

[1] Full details of these and other surveys can be found in Appendix I.

hand the majority of people not so far represented in my enquiry. This need was particularly apparent in relation to two problem areas: family composition, marriage and adoption (Survey I); and the relationship between specific variables and support for cargo cult (Survey II). In both cases quantitative data were important. It was impossible to interview all the 1,400 or so adults in the area, but it also seemed undesirable to see only those who by inclination, temperament or social position were my best informants. Therefore, in order to cover the whole area, in Surveys I and II I took a random sample (with proportionate representation for each village) from the total adult population.

A final source for villages other than Kauris was those institutions, such as church, local government council and cooperative, in which many other if not all villages participated. The written records of these organizations (together with those of the Papua New Guinea Administration) were most valuable. In addition it was possible to attend their meetings, to which came representatives of many villages.

Every fieldworker finds that he has to limit the topics on which he seeks data. I found it expedient not only to restrict myself ultimately to politics but also, from the many institutions which were politically significant, to select two for particular study. For this reason the material presented on the Ambenob Local Government Council and Yali's cargo movement is much fuller than that on other institutions.

PRESENTATION

The main body of this book is divided into three parts. Part I is intended as a background to the contemporary situation. Many elements in the traditional society survive today. Furthermore later discussion of the current role of the village will centre partly on a contrast with its traditional (pre-contact) position. Europeans first settled in Madang in the 1880s, and the second chapter in this section summarizes the main events which have taken place in the period since that decade.

One way to describe the present political scene would be to set out the functions of various corporate groups – the family, the clan, the village etc. But since the nature of corporate groups is one of the variables under scrutiny, in Part II I have chosen to present the material instead under a number of topic headings.

In successive chapters I discuss the social framework, economic activities, the conduct of public affairs, Yali's movement and the church. For each I describe the relevant corporate groups, political communities and competition for power. One criticism which could be levelled at this scheme is that it prejudices the analysis in favour of a structurally differentiated society by suggesting that each of these activities is more discrete than it actually is. However I hope that both the expediencies of data presentation and my final analysis will serve to justify this approach.

In Part III I attempt to bring the material together in an overall picture of the Madang political scene. I begin Chapter 7 with a description of certain features of the formal and functionally specialized authority structures in Madang. This rather fragmented picture is modified in the remainder of Chapter 7 and Chapter 8, which deal with leadership and political conflict respectively and indicate the relations between the separate authority structures. The discussion is concerned particularly with the current role of the traditionally autonomous village, and with the various relationships between people in different villages which result from the existence of these authority structures.

Chapters 1 to 8 are based directly on the fieldwork conducted in 1968 and 1969. No attempt has been made to modify them or add to them in the light of events since that time. However, since joining the University of Papua and New Guinea, I have had several opportunities to return to Madang, on two occasions for visits of four weeks. My Postscript 1972 does not try to summarize everything that has happened in Madang in the past three years, but looks particularly at the 1972 House of Assembly elections and the rise of political parties in the area. It is gratifying to find that the conclusions presented in Chapter 8 have considerable relevance to and explanatory value for the events of recent months.

PART I

THE BACKGROUND

I

The Traditional Way of Life[1]

Since European settlement in Madang dates from the 1880s, nobody alive today can remember what it was like before Europeans came. But many men have heard stories of earlier days or can remember their youth when the European presence had not greatly influenced their lives. They perceive elements of continuity through the many changes which have taken place, and can identify these for the enquirer. But it must be admitted that this chapter is based not on first-hand observation but on the picture of traditional society which exists in men's minds today. As such it certainly contains bias, omissions and over-simplifications which I cannot identify. The chapter will concentrate on political aspects of traditional life and here, as throughout the book, I shall not be directly concerned with political relationships within the nuclear family.

The villages under study are situated on the narrow coastal plain and on the hills which rise to about 1,500 feet immediately behind it. These hills are dissected by many deep river valleys running eastwards to the sea. There are two main seasons, wet and dry, which are brought respectively by the north-west monsoon from approximately December to April and the south-east trades from May to November. Traditionally the main crops were taro, sweet potato and yam, which were planted at the end of the dry season. A few other cultivated plants, sago, wild roots and fruits and wild and domesticated animals also contributed to the diet.

MARRIAGE AND THE FAMILY

The family, consisting of a man, his wife and their children, was the group in which children were reared and through which

[1] At the time of writing I have just completed a much more detailed account of traditional politics in Madang (Morauta (in press a)). This contains many more examples than the present account, and also refers to parallel situations in other parts of lowland Melanesia.

rights in land were acquired. Members of the elementary family did not live together. The children lived with their mothers, every woman and her children in her own house, while adult men usually ate and slept in a communal men's house. Food was collected and prepared by and for the elementary family and any dependants, such as aged relatives. Men worked together to clear and fence a garden, but the crops planted were owned and cultivated by a man and his wife. Property, apart from land, was owned and very largely inherited within the elementary family. Household goods, traditional valuables and trees which a man had himself planted were the property of individuals. One of the most important items of personal property was knowledge of magic spells. Children did not automatically inherit anything except rights in land. A man only handed on his possessions to a son who *acted* like a son. If none of his own children satisfied him, he would give his knowledge and property to the man who was most obedient and helpful to him and most solicitous of his welfare.

Most men had only one wife, but a few married dead kinsmen's wives, and the very energetic could marry two or more women on their own behalf. The ideal procedure for a first marriage was arrangement by the parents of both partners. Sometimes, however, a couple eloped or a raiding party carried off a woman to another village. A husband was in a relationship of debt to his wife's father and brother. He not only owed them brideprice, but was under a continual obligation throughout his marriage to help them with goods and services. His children too were at a disadvantage in relation to his wife's brother. They were in danger from his angry spirit (*wetu* in Kamba language), which could make them sick or lazy. When they were young their father, and later on they themselves had to be continually alert to maintain the goodwill of this man and his children. Since there was a prohibition on marriages within three generations of blood relatives of any kind, marriages were rare within the clan but common both between clans of the same village and between villages. Marriage was terminated by the death of either partner or by divorce. The children remained with the father or his clan, except when a misdemeanour on his part was held responsible for the divorce.

THE CLAN

In Madang small named patrilineal descent groups, known as *ater* in the Kamba language, regulated rights to land. It is these groups which I am calling clans. Anthropological definitions of clan and lineage have been made largely in terms of folk models, namely of those genealogical histories which informants are able to give (see Radcliffe-Brown 1950, pp. 39–40). The *ater* of Madang, although it is a functionally unitary phenomenon and always a land-holding group, takes a number of different genealogical forms. In the narrowest sense the *ater* is a group in which patrilineal links between all members and the founding ancestor are known (i.e. Radcliffe-Brown's 'lineage'). At the other extreme it is a group in which it is not possible to specify the genealogical links between all members and their founding ancestor but in which there is an ideology of common descent (i.e. Radcliffe-Brown's 'clan'). Between such polar types are other cases. Some *ater* can specify the genealogical links between all living members but cannot trace them back to their named founding ancestor. In others, the members of one branch can trace its links to the founding ancestor, while those of a different branch cannot. But all such forms are called and function as *ater*. I have decided to call such groups 'clans', firstly because to distinguish between them on a genealogical basis would not correspond either with Madang concepts or with their functions, and secondly because clanship in Radcliffe-Brown's terms could perhaps be described as the highest common factor in all these forms.[1] Although relations between some clans can be fitted into a segmentary model, in relation to one another a group of clans might have been of a variety of levels of segmentation.

The genealogies and clan histories collected indicate that non-agnates sometimes became incorporated in clans, for example when a man adopted a son or when a host gave land to a war refugee. Certainly in succeeding generations, if not in that of the newcomer himself, such non-agnates do not appear to have been overtly differentiated from true agnates, although their different

---

[1] Thus there are two possible relationships between my use of the word clan and genealogically defined lineages. Some clans were lineages, while others included one or more lineages, which might or might not have had any functional significance. Occasionally two lineages had slightly different magical duties.

origin was still remembered. Agnation was an important criterion for recruitment to clans but not the only one.

Land rights were inherited within the clan. The land of a clan might be all in one block or interdigitated with that of other clans of the same village. Ownership of land implied various rights – permanent or temporary alienation, gathering, hunting, fishing or sago-making. None of these rights could be exercised by an individual independently unless he was the only man in his clan. Each clan had a land leader, who was the senior active member. It was he whom outsiders first approached about clan land matters, but all such matters were considered by the adult men of the clan in council. The clans owned men's communal sleeping-houses, cult houses, and objects associated with the men's cult. They were distinguished from one another by their totems, legends and by the belief that certain traits of character (as well as duties) were inherited within the clan, for example a hot temper, the ability to attract women or skill in hunting.

THE VILLAGE

Clans were grouped in clusters, the composition and functions of which are discussed below. There is some difference of opinion as to whether these clusters were traditionally named or not. Informants in some villages state that the name the cluster now bears was its traditional 'address', while others say that Europeans arbitrarily chose the name of one of the constituent clans for the group as a whole. Certainly today 7 of the 17 clusters are called by the name of a constituent clan. Over time the number and combination of clans in particular villages varied because of population changes, division after a dispute, defeat in war, natural disasters or annihilation supposedly as a punishment for disregard of the rules of the men's cult.

In Kamba language this cluster of clans is known as *kapa*, in Pidgin as *piles* and in English (among the few Madangs who speak it) as 'village'. The churches, the Administration and the local government council follow this Pidgin and English usage. The term *kapa* appears to have a geographical as well as a social referent. Frequently people say *da kapa atina*, I am going to the village. However, the village was not a compact residential unit, although members of one village were likely to build closer to one another than to outsiders. Hogbin and Wedgwood have argued against the use of the term 'village' for such social groups because 'it suggests a degree of centralization, both of buildings and social life, which is by no means always found' (1953, p. 253). In its place they suggest 'parish', a term which they define as 'the largest local group forming a political unit' (1953, p. 243). As we shall see, the Madang clan cluster is certainly a parish in this sense. However, I prefer to use the term 'village' because I consider that Hogbin and Wedgwood's arguments do not have the force in this case that they may have elsewhere. In Madang the village had identifiable social as well as political functions and usually some degree of compactness. Moreover, the vernacular term has both social and geographical referents. Finally, I conducted my fieldwork in a situation in which the English term 'village' had already become standard usage.

THE COMPOSITION AND FUNCTIONS OF THE VILLAGE

According to legend the commonest reason why two or more clans combined in a single village was that they were linked by patrilineal descent. The founding ancestors of several clans might have been brothers, or one clan might have split off from another. Sometimes there was no detailed genealogical account, but a tradition of 'one blood' or a story of ancestors travelling together from distant parts to their present home. But although there was a patrilineally recruited core of clans in each village, there could also have been some clans whose membership had another origin. Where clans separated, especially after warfare or quarrels, they might have left their home village and moved to join another cluster. Legends describe two modes of incorporation of strangers: either they were adopted into and became members of an existing clan or they were given a separate piece of land and became a clan in their own right. Neither at clan nor village level was there any obvious use of genealogical fictions to make the past correspond with the present. Informants were very ready with stories of quarrels, departures, adoptions, exiles, routs etc. They readily acknowledged the 'foreign' origin of certain member clans, but such a history did not imply any limitations on land rights. Patrilineal descent was only one of a number of ways in which clans validated their ultimate title to land.

Clans in a single village owned adjacent land, and a clan owned land in one village only. It is clear that for those whose holdings were interspersed with those of other clans, a permanent defensive alliance with the latter was imperative. But in villages where each clan had a single block of land, fringe clans would have had as many boundaries in common with a neighbouring village as with their own.

Map 1. Location of the 17 villages under study

The residential pattern within a single village was (and is) more complicated than Map 1 would suggest. Usually only one or two clans lived in a single settlement (and sometimes a single clan could be divided between two). The main reason for forming larger settlements was probably the danger of sudden attack; those clans which were numerically stronger were able to live in greater isolation. The scanty information obtainable on marriages of parents or grandparents of the senior surviving generation suggests that a considerable number were made within the village.

The village was the largest political unit, the largest permanent corporate group which made decisions for itself or on behalf of which decisions were made. Its political organization rested on two institutions: the men's cult and individually owned magic. These two institutions embodied respectively two important political notions: rule by consensus and spheres of responsibility.

THE MEN'S CULT AND RULE BY CONSENSUS

The men's cult centred on cult houses (*barag darem* in Kamba language, *haus tambaran* today in Pidgin). In Madang these are to be distinguished from the men's houses in which adult men ate and slept. Usually each clan had its own cult house, but if a clan was too small to build and operate one on its own it would combine with another, and a junior segment or a subsidiary of another clan might share a cult house. The *barag darem* was a large 'A'-frame house with each end completely sealed except for one door. Sacred items such as stones, gourds, short spears, flutes and bull-roarers were kept in it. At festival times some of these objects would be taken to a special site in the forest and then returned in a ceremonial fashion to the house. Thereafter there would be several nights of feasting and dancing before the sacred paraphernalia were once again returned to the forest (and ultimately in secrecy back to the cult house).

Women and children were excluded from the cult house at all times. Young men were initiated into the cult at the age of about 20, when they were shown the sacred objects and permitted to enter the house. After initiation they were allowed to marry, but in other respects their growth in status was slow. It was only gradually that the older men taught them the meaning of the ritual and the clan legends and totems. It was only gradually, too, that a man would hand over his magic and personal property to his heir. Young males were socially females and so excluded from the cult until their formal initiation. The men's cult was not directed to specific ends such as fertile gardens, good weather or success in war, but to the general welfare of the clan. Nor was the men's cult in any way private within the adult male clan community. A man visiting his affines in another village could enter their cult house and join in their celebrations. Frequently other clans helped one clan in their village in the ceremonies, and dancing and initiation was organized by the village, not by the clan or the individual family.

Informants describe the men's cult as their forefathers' local government council, their House of Assembly. In each men's cult house the adult men met in clan or, more inclusively, village councils. At the clan level, as far as adult men were concerned, this was not representative government but direct democracy; all were formally of equal standing in the meeting. The council or meeting was called *tamaniak* (Kamba language). The word also had the meaning 'all together' and was used to report decisions in the form 'we, the meeting of X clan, have decided...'. The term also referred to the fact that decisions were reached by consensus. At a meeting everyone had to have his say, nobody could go unheard, no opinion unexpressed. Anger, resentment or interested motives should not be hidden. Unspoken reservations were believed to be dangerous to the person who did not speak out and to cause sickness in him or his family. Gradually a majority view would emerge, but nobody in the minority could be over-ruled. So the discussion would go backwards and forwards until unanimity was achieved. A man would not say he was defeated. He would say 'They pressed me, and I said, never mind, I'll fall in with your plans.' If he verbally yielded but really did not, it was believed that he would suffer for his deceit. Thus, as informants recognized, a stubborn man could exercise a veto on a course of action supported by everyone else. It also followed from the democratic principle that no individual could make a decision for the group.

The supporting sanction for rule by consensus was the great value set on harmony in the community. There was an ideal of peace which was 'broken' by quarrels, gossip, resentment and hidden malice. Concealed ill-will was believed to be automatically punished by supernatural sanctions, and open hostility invited reprisals in the form of physical attack and sorcery. When the peace (in Kamba language *maror*, in Pidgin *lo*) was destroyed, it could only be restored by the public confession of anger and grudges. Then people would join in a feast and exchange gifts, once again making themselves of 'one heart'.

The size of the units seeking consensus was probably relatively small. The earliest population figures available, for 1944, cover only 12 of the villages. In that year villages averaged only 105 people altogether and, calculating from contemporary clan numbers, 14 clans only. The politically active community was even smaller, since it excluded females and uninitiated males. In 1944 this would have given an average of five politically active members per clan. The effective size of the unit within which consensus was sought was further reduced by the fact that younger men deferred to the views of their fathers and seniors.

All issues were discussed first at a clan meeting. Village meetings were held in the cult house of one of the member clans (although sometimes less formal gatherings were held). Land matters were the concern solely of the clan, but initiation, gardening activities, trading expeditions, misdemeanours and disputes within and between villages were discussed at both levels. In the field of social control the *tamaniak* was only one element in a wider system which also included automatic supernatural sanctions and physical and magical self-help. In inter-village disputes a man whose daughter had been abducted or garden destroyed could bring his grievance to his own *tamaniak* if he wanted to. Only if his complaint appeared justified, or his fellow members had other reasons for agreeing would the clan or village be mobilized for war. Within the village the *tamaniak* could discuss a quarrel or misdemeanour if it was asked to. The rights and wrongs of the matter were debated and suggestions made for compensation. It appears also that the *tamaniak* could employ sorcery against one of its number.

INDIVIDUALLY OWNED MAGIC AND SPHERES OF RESPONSIBILITY

Whereas land was owned by the clan, property of other kinds including magic was owned individually. This magic could be acquired by inheritance (see p. 12) or purchased for pots and pigs. It was also possible for new magic to be discovered in dreams or visions. Certain types of magic could be hired, but in such cases the hirer would not be taught the secret spell. One form of individually owned magic was that which was considered essential for certain community activities: initiation into the men's cult; peacemaking and feast giving; warfare (there was magic for firing men's minds to battle and for preparing their weapons);

the start each year of new gardens; the preparation of the soil and taro tops; the first harvesting of wild fruits in the forest; and the hunting of pigs with nets.

These types of magic, all vital to the community as a whole, were distributed between clans in such a way that each was dependent on the rest for the specialist magic which it did not itself own. Responsibility rested with the 'owning' individual or clan. In all 16 villages for which information was available the clan which would have traditionally owned the war magic could be identified. In 13 of these the clan which was responsible for peace-keeping and hospitality (for looking after the *maror* in Kamba, in Pidgin the *lo*) could also be identified. In five others gardening clans were remembered, and many other magical specialisms belonged to only one or two clans in certain villages. Here are the traditional clan specializations in Kauris village:

Bara	fighting
Bara Kumi	a subsidiary of Bara
Bawewe	a subsidiary of Krualgug
Kauris	feasts and hospitality
Krualgug	dances and love
Lawel	gardens, especially taro
Menmarpi	some food and wild fruits

In no village was the war-making clan also responsible for peace-keeping, but in several instances one clan had more than one duty. Many clans had special kinds of magic (e.g. for love) which were not significant for communal village undertakings but neverthe-less played an important part in the clan's image and traditions. This division of magical labour (in combination with historical precedence in a village) seems to have conferred on certain clans what can be best described as 'submerged rank', though it should be stressed that this was not based on any ascribed political or economic precedence. The political influence exerted by a clan at any one time depended on its numerical strength and the ability of its senior men. It seems that there was often competition between clans for this *de facto* supremacy.[1]

---

[1] Somewhat similar patterns of specialisation among sub-groups of larger political units have been recorded for several other areas of lowland Melanesia, especially by Meiser (1955, p. 369) for the Kaean people near the mouth of the Ramu River, by Malinowski (1922, pp. 398–9, 409, 411) for the Trobriands, by

Magic spells were owned by individuals, yet informants say 'X clan were the warriors' or 'Y clan were the gardeners'. So we must ask: in what sense was the clan as a whole involved? Although at any particular time the magic was in the hands of one man, it was inherited largely within the clan, both because men in it were close kinsmen and lived and worked together and because the spells themselves often consisted of ancestral names. Magic spells could also be connected with a clan as a whole because they were associated with clan property or land, clan sacred places, clan legends and history or clan totems. Some informants say that clans were specialized in their daily activities: the warriors patrolled the fringes of the settlement while the gardeners gardened. It seems more likely that this was a matter of circumstances; in all-out war most people would certainly have been in arms. But it is clear that, while not actually knowing the spells themselves, clan members could assist their magician in his work. Thus when hospitality was offered in the men's house of a hospitality clan, all members would have contributed food and delicacies to the meal.

At times when concerted action was needed the magicians provided leadership – not so much in the making of the decision, but in the manner of the doing. Although the particular man varied from one context to another, there was always someone to appoint a day to clear the garden, organize tactics for a fight or supervise preparations for a feast. Since the community depended on the magician, he could assert himself by refusing cooperation, more often by delaying action than by a direct veto. Magicians were sometimes believed to have magic to influence the course of discussions. Many war magicians secretly spat spells on the areca nuts which were to be chewed during the debate in the belief that this would fire men's hearts for war.

LEADERSHIP

So far I have mentioned the land leader, who held his position as the senior active member of his clan, and the magician leader who gained his position by selective inheritance. Both these men

Young (1971, pp. 62–6) for Goodenough Island, by Hau'ofa (1971, pp. 155, 159) for the Mekeo, by Seligman (1910, p. 281) for the Roro and by Williams (1936, pp. 73–4) for the Keraki of the Trans-Fly. These are discussed in detail elsewhere – see p. 11 n.1.

C

could be said to hold office, the first by ascription and the second by a mixture of ascription and achievement. But there were others who were influential in the village through the nature and force of their own personality. These were the people who were known locally, as elsewhere in New Guinea, as Big Men (*danah nari* in Kamba language, *bikpela man* in Pidgin). Several traits of character, either singly or in combination, could bring a man to prominence. A man could have physical strength and courage and be easily roused to fight; he could be full of ideas and articulate in discussion; he could be wise in handling disputes and in making peace between angry men; or he could be generous with gifts and, because of his widespread credit, be able to organize large feasts and presentations. There was no reason why these characteristics should coincide (a man who was a keen fighter was not likely to be also a good peacemaker). In this sphere of achieved prominence men competed with one another; but magician leaders because of their limited spheres of interest normally did not.

There was no office of Big Man; this was an entirely *optional* role. Sometimes a clan or village had no such prominent men, but corporate decisions could still be taken within the framework of consensus, and activities run smoothly under the supervision of the specialist magicians. At other times there were several prominent men within a small group. The Big Men did not constitute the political system. They were not even indispensable to it. Where they existed, Big Men *did* have significance as politicians, but only as politicians acting within the framework of consensus. They came to prominence by realizing or attempting to realize certain Madang ideals of behaviour incorporated in which were various limitations on their influence. For example, a fighter was not respected if he wanted to fight when others did not, and a successful orator or mediator had to listen to public opinion and respond to it. Anyone who tried to push himself too far forward and increase his own influence at the expense of others ran the risk of making enemies, being attacked by sorcery and being harmed by the angry spirits (*wetu*) of those who were hostile to him. Within these limits talented men could exert their influence in debate and private discussion and through the creation of relationships of economic dependence.

In practice the same men often operated simultaneously in the formal and informal leadership systems. Any man at some time during his life was likely to be the senior active member and therefore automatically the land leader of his clan. The magician leaders, selected as they were by their predecessors, would have been chosen because they embodied the prized virtues of obedience and generosity, were social conformers and perhaps even showed some aptitude for their particular magical duties. Thus a war magician would choose the more courageous of his sons as his successor. In turn a successful magician would have more influence than an unsuccessful one. When one man combined ascriptive position with other grounds for leadership his influence was so great that it was decisive not only within his village but in the balance of power between villages. Such a man was Malok of Mis, who was prominent in the 1870s and 1880s. He was the magician of the hospitality and peacemaking clan, renowned for his personal generosity and his wise decisions. Malok's time, Mis people say, was a good time, a time of unanimity in the village and of peace with neighbours. But the system did not depend on the presence of such men. The great Malok was followed in Mis by a period when its magicians were of no particular repute. At both times the village was a viable unit with exactly the same formal political structure.

INTER-VILLAGE RELATIONSHIPS

Some villages within a geographically compact language group (see Map 2) were linked by ties of patrilineal descent of the same order as those between clans within a village; sometimes their ties were of a less well-defined nature. For example, the four original Kamba-speaking villages were believed to have been founded by four brothers, whose descendants formed the patrilineal core of each. Not all villages of one language group could trace such ties, although most had some kind of common history. In addition there was a type of village grouping called Big Name (e.g. Big Name Wagi, Big Name Fuar etc.). Within a Big Name area a common body of custom was thought to prevail, and its boundaries were defined by the criteria of language, history and territory, not always coincident. But neither language nor Big Name groups formed corporate political units with common leaders, councils or functions.

Nevertheless there was considerable contact between villages in various contexts. Informal markets were held at which the special products of different areas were traded. For example, fish and lime were mainly available on the coast, while some crops grew more abundantly, or only grew at all, in the cooler hill-country. Certain villages also enjoyed craft monopolies; clay pots, for instance, were made only in Butelkud in the area

Map 2. Languages of the 17 villages

under study and in Yabob and Bilbil on the coast. From much further afield (Karkar Island and the Rai Coast) came drums, certain kinds of nut, wooden plates and bark belts. Market-days were arranged by adjacent villages, although others could attend. There was a strict rule that two non-adjacent villages could only trade through an intervening one. At markets goods were exchanged directly and not necessarily between kinsmen or trading partners, though they could carry on delayed exchange when they met there. By trading with their coastal neighbours the Madang villagers were able to acquire goods obtained in the long-distance sea trading voyages of, for example, the Krankets and Bilbils (see also Harding 1967).

Village also encountered village in warfare. On the whole villages fought as units under their war magicians, but sometimes a particularly independent clan would not join in. People who had relatives among the enemy, although not disloyal to the point of treachery, might refuse to take part in a fight, or would avoid a hand-to-hand encounter with their kinsmen. Alliances were formed for particular wars, allies being either whole villages, single clans or individuals. Such alliances might be based on personal ties, common grudges or the prospect of excitement and reward. Informants gave as the main causes of war: land, women and pigs.

By far the most important inter-personal ties between villages were those created by marriage. Although genealogical data cannot yield an accurate picture of the pre-contact pattern of marriages, it is possible to identify one or two trends. Marriages were most common between near or neighbouring villages, and there was some imbalance in the flows of women towards, and away from the coast. Although Madang women married Austronesian-speaking men, the reverse was not the case (nor did I record one case of this today). This is probably associated with ecological and cultural (notably perceived hygienic) differences. Similarly women from Gal and Matepi villages (immediately west of Opi) married in Kauris to the east, but Kauris women did not move so far westwards. This was explained by the arduous life of women in higher country. Despite what has been said (pp. 12, 17) on the importance of intra-village marriage in traditional times, we should not underestimate the significance of marriage ties for relationships between villages – for alliance in war, for the betrayal of ambushes, for participation in life-cycle rituals and men's cult celebrations and for the purchase, hire and trading of goods and such services as sorcery, assassination, divination and healing. Villages were also linked by ties between trading partners, who were not necessarily kinsmen. Partners built up relationships of mutual indebtedness and hospitality over a number of years, and these were inherited from one generation to the next.

Although villages were politically autonomous, there was very considerable uniformity in social and cultural usages throughout Madang. Despite the multiplicity of languages, the men's cult, the obligations of kinsmen and the performance of leaders (for example) were relatively constant throughout the area. Although there were no political units which included several villages, there was in some sense an inter-village *moral* community. Not only did all villagers in the area live their lives in the same institutional framework but relationships between them were governed by recognized rules. In person-to-person ties, both within and between villages, few distinctions were made on grounds of village membership. An affine was an affine wherever he came from. Brideprice was paid to the wife's father whether he was in a man's own village or another. Specialist services were hired in the same manner whether within or between villages. The fear of sorcery, which reinforced social norms within the village, operated in the same way outside it. Trading was governed by shared expectations; for instance, there were accepted norms relating to the inheritance of partnerships, the conduct of delayed exchange, value and equivalence and the right of one village to trade with another. In the same way many villages had mutual agreements about common land boundaries and, in addition, land could be purchased, given or lent according to widely accepted principles. There was a sense in which all villages were jointly responsible for the preservation of the *tambaran* cult. Breach of its secrecy rules in one village was said to be punishable by the joint action of neighbouring villages, who were supposed to combine and wipe out the offenders. There were also accepted methods for concluding hostilities in time of war.

These norms were not enforced by any formal institutions. They were sanctioned by the threat of sorcery, fear of supernatural forces, warfare and the possibility of loss of trade and safe conduct. Affines and trade friends sometimes mediated in hostilities. There was no institutionalized boundary to this inter-village moral community; there was no cut-off point beyond which no holds or fewer holds were barred. Villagers probably recognized, as they do today, differences of local custom in more distant areas. But the norms and sanctions which governed inter-village relationships did not operate in a limited community but in a social universe which, to those within it, appeared to fade gradually away into the distant mountains.

2

From 1871 to the Present Day

Although exploration of the north coast of New Guinea began with the Portuguese and Spanish navigators of the sixteenth century, it was not until 1871 that the first European settled there and became known to local people. This was the Russian scientist and explorer Baron Mikloucho-Maclay, who made three visits to the Bogadjim area (about 17 miles south of Madang) between 1871 and 1883 (Fischer 1955). During his stay Maclay made several trips farther north to where Madang Town now stands.

In 1885 the pioneers of the German New Guinea Company landed in the present-day Morobe District (Flierl 1931, p. 117), and in the next decade stations and plantations were established at other points along the coast, including one called Friedrich Wilhelmshafen on the site of today's township of Madang. From 1892 to 1899 the headquarters of the company was at Friedrich Wilhelmshafen (Lawrence 1964, p. 37). After passing from German to Australian hands in 1914 (ultimately under a League of Nations mandate), much of New Guinea was occupied by the Japanese in the Second World War, Madang Town itself being taken without a battle in December 1942. The Japanese withdrew from Madang in 1944, and since that time the Territory of New Guinea has been in Australian hands, from 1946 as a Trust Territory of the United Nations. In 1949 an administrative union was created with the Australian territory of Papua.

It was not until 1964 that the first national elections for a representative parliament were held on a universal franchise. The second House of Assembly, elected in 1968, consisted of 69 members for Open and 15 for larger Regional electorates, plus 10 official members. Candidates for Regional electorates had to have the Territory Intermediate Certificate, but no educational qualifications were required for Open candidates (Hughes, C. A., 1965, p. 36). In 1968 the villages under study belonged to the Mabuso Open and the Madang Regional electorates. The Administration appointed Ministerial and Assistant Ministerial Members from among the elected representatives, and in 1968 Mr Angmai Bilas, M.H.A. for Mabuso Open, held the portfolio of Trade and Industry. Several national political parties have appeared since 1961, but by 1968/69 only two, the All People's Party and the Country Party (see Wolfers 1967, pp. 29–30), had any connection with Madang District and no villagers in the area under study had joined either. Indeed no local informants knew anything about them. By 1972 the situation had changed radically; these recent developments are discussed in Postscript 1972 (pp. 163–9).

The first official German patrol visited Nobanob, Kamba, Opi and Korog in 1906 (Imperial German Government 1906, pp. 15–17). From the time of this first contact the Germans recognized the village as an important unit of social organization and made it the base unit for the appointment of local officials. In each village they appointed a *luluai* or headman and a *tultul*, an assistant headman or village policeman (Rowley 1954, p. 774). From April 1911 about eight of the villages under study were liable to an annual head tax of 5 marks (Imperial German Government 1911, p. 118). In 1904 the Germans extended to Madang the policy of increasing the size of administrative units by combining villages in 'unions' under a single *luluai*. Under the Australians there was again one *luluai* for each village, and their total number greatly increased (Rowley 1954, pp. 775–6). Later paramount *luluai* were appointed over very much wider areas than the old German unions, the first in Madang being Giri of Kauris. The nearest other paramount *luluai* were in the Bogadjim area to the south, and on Karkar Island 40 miles by sea to the north-east. In 1946/47 there were 375 *luluai* and 330 *tultul* under these three paramount *luluai* (D.D.A., Annual Report, Madang District, 1946/47).

In 1940 the Administration encouraged the establishment of councils in a few individual villages. After the war these were revived (D.D.A., Annual Report, Madang District, 1946/47), and in 1950 they were extended to cover several villages, though only one of those under study, Kesup, was involved in this scheme (D.D.A., Special Report of A. D. O. Keenan, 21 January 1951). In 1956 the Ambenob Native Local Government Council finally replaced the system of administration through *luluai* and *tultul*. From its inception this council covered all the villages under study as well as some others. Its boundaries have been extended several times; in 1956 it served a population of 10,000, and in the early part of 1969 it covered 17,000 people (D.D.A., Local Government Councils in New Guinea, File 42-4-2). Villagers were now liable for council tax and the Administration head tax was abolished. In 1969 Ambenob Council became 'Multi-Racial', that is to say its authority and its electorate included residents of plantations, schools etc. The council is responsible for minor public works (the installation of pumps, building of secondary roads and classrooms etc.) and for some recurrent expenses incurred by the provision of medical and educational services and roads in its area. A local government adviser, an expatriate public servant, is attached to the council and through him or more directly the various Government departments make suggestions and recommendations. In 1957 District Advisory Councils were also established with a nominated membership consisting mainly of expatriates and a minority of indigenes (Parker 1966, p. 251). Members are appointed for two years and meetings are held quarterly. Since 1962, 8 of the 15 members of the Madang D.A.C. have been indigenes and have been entitled to submit items for the agenda. In 1968/69 the President of Ambenob Council was one of these. All councils in the Madang District send representatives to an annual District Conference, and a national Association of Local Government Councils also holds regular meetings.

The legal system contains elements of arbitration as well as a formal hierarchy of courts. Within the village there is room for arbitration, and it can also be exercised by local government councillors, patrol officers and welfare workers employed by the Administration. In the hierarchy of courts the lowest is the Local Court presided over by either an Administration official acting as magistrate or a full-time magistrate. This sits occasionally in a village but more frequently in Madang Town. In 1968/69 the Local Court magistrate in Madang was a Papua New Guinean. The District Court is presided over by a stipendiary magistrate permanently posted to Madang, and the Supreme Court by judges in circuit. Although the legal code mainly follows that of Queensland, provision is made in some ordinances for the recognition of indigenous custom (Commonwealth of Australia 67/68, p. 47).

In the German period a large area of land was alienated for the township, and for the extensive commercial plantations of the New Guinea Company and other foreign enterprises. Freehold rights granted in that period are still valid. Under present Australian legislation land may not be alienated to non-indigenes. The latter may however lease land which has been acquired by the Administration. Today only 5 of the 17 villages (Kauris, Mirkuk, Mukuru, Urugan and Yahil) have lost none of their land. The villages most affected are Foran (966 acres alienated), Mis (814 acres) and Nobanob (4,251 acres).[1] In many villages land has also been transferred from customary tenure for schemes such as schools and the Ambenob Cocoa Project (see below) which serve villagers themselves.

Under the Land Titles Commission Ordinance 1962–7, a commission was created to ascertain and register indigenous rights in land (Commonwealth of Australia 67/68, p. 68). The local arm of this commission is a Local Demarcation Committee, appointed for an Adjudication Area covering a group of villages. It consists of one member for each clan in every village of the area, with a chairman who has no land interest within it. For each village there is a vice-chairman elected by and from among the clan representatives who helps to coordinate discussions at the village level. In cases of dispute, reference is made to higher officials and if all else fails to a formal hearing by a Commissioner who is empowered to give a decision.

Individual tenure can be acquired in a number of ways. Under the Land (Tenure Conversion) Ordinance 1963–7 communally owned land may be converted into individually owned blocks, and temporary rights individually registered can be acquired in the form of Clan Land Use Agreements. In Madang land acquired by the Administration for the Ambenob Cocoa Project is leased to individual cocoa growers.

The Germans built a number of roads in Madang, including one from Friedrich Wilhelmshafen to Sek, another to the Gum River and one in the Hansemann mountains near and behind Nobanob. These roads fell into disrepair under Australian administration in the pre-war period, but since 1945 there has

---

[1] This information is taken from Department of Lands, Surveys and Mines, Fourmil and Milinch (1965) series and 10 chain (1971) series of maps; also Minutes of the Territory Lands Board.

been an upsurge in road building. By 1968/69, 13 of the 17 villages under study had at least one major settlement within 15 minutes' walk of a vehicular road.

From the mid-1930s the policy of the Australian Administration was to develop large communal vegetable or rice gardens, usually involving more than one village. In the 1950s various problems encountered with these earlier schemes led to a change in method, and cooperative societies were started. These processed and marketed produce grown independently by individual villagers. Bel and Pau societies in 1968 and 1964 respectively included among their members 114 people from 15 of the 17 Madang villages.[1] Both these societies foundered because of organizational difficulties and the existence of alternative outlets for produce. Today the Madang Cocoa Cooperative (with 98 members from 14 Madang villages in March 1968) is the only such organization to survive in the area under study. It is concerned entirely with the drying and marketing of cocoa beans for which the small producer has no alternative outlet. Each group of villages has a director on the board, and annual general meetings are open to all members. This cooperative is one of several making up the District-wide Madang Association of Native Societies, which organizes bulk buying and storage.

Today the Administration's policy seems to be to encourage individual production and selling. Development Bank Loans are available for what are considered to be commercially viable projects such as coconut planting and cattle raising. Technical and commercial advice is given by the Department of Agriculture, Stock and Fisheries, the Division of District Administration and the Business Advisory Service (established in Madang in 1969). By hiring cheap labour from more backward areas producers can become independent of their clan and village and some, as was just mentioned, have acquired individual land rights.

Today a variety of cash-earning activities are open to those who elect to remain in the villages. Copra can be sold in large quantities to the Copra Marketing Board or in smaller quantities to various other buyers. Coffee is grown on a small scale. A considerable amount of cocoa is produced and sold to the cooperative by both members and non-members. In 1967/68,

[1] These and subsequent figures are taken from Department of Agriculture, Stock and Fisheries (D.A.S.F.), registers of members for each society.

87,935 lb. of wet beans were sold to the cooperative by 14 of the 17 villages (D.A.S.F., 'Production Madang Central, 1967-8', File 38-2A (1)). The small quantity of rice which is produced is sold directly to D.A.S.F. In 1968/69 there were fewer than six cattle-owners in Madang, but several men were wiring cleared areas in preparation for the arrival of new cattle. Landowners can sometimes sell stands of timber, as well as firewood and gravel. In the 17 villages there are at least 27 small trade stores, most of them stocking kerosene and a very limited range of foods with highly informal 'shop' arrangements. Six trucks or utilities are operated commercially by Madang residents. But market gardening is still the most common cash earner, and 68 per cent of Madang men regularly receive income from this source (Survey II). Although some produce is sold at the Catholic Mission station at Sek and to various urban institutions, most is taken to the market in Madang Town. Established originally in 1937 and reopened after the war, the market is open on Tuesdays, Thursdays and Saturdays. During a four-week survey conducted in December/January 1968/69, I found that 939 sellers attended the market from the Madang villages though at least some of these would have been foreigners resident in the area. Madang market is also important for the present study because it acts as a centre for the distribution of information and gossip over a wide area of the Madang District. During the four weeks of the survey, sellers attended from approximately 200 different villages or areas. On the journey to market too kinsmen are visited and news exchanged. People from six different villages join trucks at the two road-head villages of Barahaim and Kauris, many of them sleeping overnight in a village near the road ready for the dawn truck journey to town.

Until 1941 there was no Government-run school in Madang District, and all education for indigenous people was in the hands of the missions. Today in the Madang villages 45 per cent of the population under 16 is enrolled in primary schools, and others are in high schools.[1] Of these about 75 per cent are in Government-run schools. Primary schools and the Administration's

[1] These figures are based on school registers made available by the Department of Education, Lutheran Mission, Madang and the Seventh Day Adventist Mission and on Ambenob Local Government Council (A.L.G.C.), Village Census Sheets, 1967.

Tusbab High School in Madang Town have Parents and Citizens' Associations which hold regular meetings, raise funds and provide labour for school improvements. Medical services in the area are provided by council and mission-sponsored medical aid posts and a mobile clinic for children and expectant mothers. Villagers take more serious cases to one of the three hospitals in or relatively near Madang Town. Various measures for environmental sanitation have also been introduced, including the use of cemeteries and deep-pit latrines. Ambenob Council's Health Committee makes tours of inspection in villages and has powers to fine offenders against the various hygiene rules.

As can be seen from Table 2, approximately 46 per cent of adult males in Madang are Lutherans, 2 per cent are Roman Catholics and 1 per cent are Seventh Day Adventists. The Lutheran and Catholic missions both arrived in the area before the turn of the century and, by mutual agreement, have worked largely in separate areas. Seventh Day Adventists came immediately after the Second World War, and the Jehovah's Witnesses, though they have not at present any adherents in the Madang villages, have been active in the area in recent years (for example in Korog in 1958 and 1959). After a slow start the Lutherans obtained large-scale conversions so that by the end of the 1930s many people from all 17 villages had been baptized. Since then however the church has lost ground, and now there are 10 Madang villages where there are no Christians or where they are in the minority. Today the mission form of organization has been replaced by a democratic and indigenous-run church known as the Evangelical Lutheran Congregation of New Guinea (E.L.C.O.N.G.). Within this there are village elders, congregational committees and circuit and district councils. These are concerned not only with spiritual matters but with the disposal of funds, the training, placing and welfare of workers, church buildings, schools and medical aid posts. In many villages there are no church buildings, but services are held in private houses and many individuals follow the Lutheran tradition of family prayer. The Lutherans have encouraged cash cropping, not only for the benefit of church funds but to raise the local standard of living. In 1959, in further pursuit of this aim, the Lutheran Mission founded NAMASU (see Fairbairn 1969), a largely indigenously owned company, financially and organizationally separate from

the Mission itself. In Madang NAMASU sells goods wholesale
to trade stores, purchases copra and coffee and hires out transport
to rural producers.

Apart from the alienation of land, one of the most important
influences of the expatriate-dominated private sector of the
economy has been the demand for labour. Before the Second
World War most labour was indentured and many Madangs
had their first taste of life outside the village when working on
the plantations of coastal and island New Guinea. Today Madangs

Table 2. Mission/Yali affiliation of adult males resident in Madang Sub-District

Village	Lutheran	Roman Catholic	S.D.A.	All church-goers	Yali	Neither attend church nor support Yali	Other
Barahaim	8	—	—	8	6	39	5
Butelkud	10	6	—	16	9	4	—
Foran	24	—	1	25	—	3	—
Haidurem	34	1	—	35	—	—	—
Kamba	25	—	—	25	57	6	4
Kauris	17	—	—	17	18	3	1
Kesup	2	1	—	3	37	1	1
Korog	11	—	—	11	28	15	1
Mirkuk	—	—	—	—	37	3	—
Mis	40	—	—	40	—	4	—
Mukuru	25	4	—	29	—	2	1
Nobanob	110	—	—	110	—	7	—
Opi	2	—	—	2	13	5	—
Panim	5	—	7	12	5	11	—
Silabob	19	—	—	19	2	3	—
Urugan	3	—	—	3	22	2	2
Yahil	—	—	—	—	10	—	—
Totals	335	12	8	355	244	108	15
Percentages	46·4	1·66	1·11	49·1	33·7	15·0	2·08

Source: Survey III.

Notes: 1. Nobanob figures are approximate. A few people were omitted from su
2. 'Other' consists of 12 cases where affiliation was not recorded, two mentally def
men and one who said he was both a Roman Catholic (when at school) and a suppor
Yali (when at home).

prefer to work for wages in the country's rapidly expanding towns. In 1966 Madang Town itself had a population of nearly 9,000 (Commonwealth of Australia 67/68, p. 202) and by 1971, partly because its boundaries were extended, this had risen to nearly 16,000 (Department of the Administrator, Bureau of Statistics). There appears to be a tendency particularly for unskilled workers to migrate to this, their nearest town. Thus in 1968 30 per cent of the indigenous residents of Madang Town came from the Madang Sub-District (Tusbab High School 1968, Table 2.0).

Today all Madang villages have people living away from their homes; about 24 per cent of the men are absent, as Table 3 shows. This table includes those in schools or colleges, unemployed

Table 3. Numbers of men absent from their villages

Village	Total no. adult males	Absent and resident within Madang	Absent and resident outside Sub-District	Total absent	Total absent (%)
Barahaim	72	5	14	19	26·4
Butelkud	33	5	4	9	27·9
Foran	36	3	8	11	30·6
Haidurem	36	8	1	9	25·0
Kamba	101	16	9	25	24·5
Kauris	46	4	7	11	23·9
Kesup	44	8	2	10	22·7
Korog	62	6	7	13	21·0
Mirkuk	47	11	7	18	38·3
Mis	51	2	7	9	17·6
Mukuru	34	6	2	8	23·5
Nobanob	133	not known	16	not known	—
Opi	20	2	—	2	10·0
Panim	30	1	2	3	10·0
Silabob	27	—	3	3	11·1
Urugan	33	6	4	10	30·3
Yahil	12	—	2	2	16·7
Totals*	684	83	79	162	
Percentages*	100	12·1	11·6	23·7	

* Excluding Nobanob.

Source: Survey III.

Notes: 1. All figures for Nobanob not available.
2. The figure for Mirkuk is abnormally high because many men live in neighbouring villages owing to their fear of sorcery at home.
3. Madang Town falls within Madang Sub-District.

as well as employed and those who, for various reasons, live in villages other than their own. There is a considerable turnover in the actual people who are absent. Thus all 56 men for whom the information was available, and who were not at the time in full-time education, had been in employment outside the village for some period during their lives (Survey II). Commonly young single men go away for a few years before settling down with a wife and family. However, the more skilled the worker the longer he is likely to stay away, and the more likely he is to raise a family in town. Men from several Madang villages commute daily to Madang Town, and others work as part-time stevedores when work is available on the wharfs. In 1960 the Madang and Foreign Workers' Council (later the Madang Workers' Association) was formed (see Stevenson 1968). Madang villagers in fluctuating numbers join the Stevedores Branch of this association and participate in its affairs.

HISTORY OF MADANG CARGO CULTS[1]

In this book I am concerned more with the political implications of cargo cults than with the reason why they arise. That is not to imply that these or any cults are purely political movements and I do not see my account as in conflict with Peter Lawrence's very valuable analysis (1964) of the epistemological background in the southern Madang District as a whole. The cults described in this section have not appeared in all the 17 villages under study. Their incidence is indicated in Table 4 (in which an X indicates the occurrence of a cult). Several of the cults described occurred also in villages outside the area of study. I have first-hand knowledge of only two. For the majority I am repeating folk history and have had no control over what events are remembered or reported by informants.

Although E. F. Hannemann (personal communication) says that by 1924 some of the coastal villagers were trying to make money by magic, Madang informants do not recall specifically cargo-oriented ritual before the late 1930s. However, they do remember a number of rather mystical and to them very significant events. I describe one of these to set the scene and also because it seems likely that it may well have had cargo implications that are now

---

[1] Material in this and other sections on Yali's organization has already been published in a slightly different form in Morauta 1972b.

forgotten: I was told that about the year 1934 a special areca
nut wrapped in a bread-fruit leaf and tied to a twig was passed
carefully from village to village. The nut was known as Elias
(the Biblical Elijah). Originally it had been picked from a
magical clump of palms, and was intended to kill a certain mission

4. Village distribution of cargo cults (at least one resident member participating)

| | | | Cults | | | | | |
| | | | Yali | | | Yakob | | Yali |
lage	Tagarab	Letub	Camps	Owro	Kaumaip	I	II	1968
aim	X	X	X (K)	X	X	X	—	X
kud	—	X	X (K)	—	—	X	—	X
	—	X	X (B)	—	X	—	—	—
arem	—	X	X (N)	—	—	X	—	—
a	X	X	X (K)	—	—	—	X	X
s	X	X	X (K)	X	—	—	X	X
o	X	—	X (Ya)	—	X	X	—	X
g	X	X	X (K)	X	—	—	—	X
ik	X	—	X (B & K)	X	X	X	—	X
	X	X	—	—	—	—	—	—
aru	—	X	X (M)	—	—	—	—	—
nob	—	X	X (N)	—	—	X	—	—
	—	X	X (K)	—	—	X	—	X
a	X	X	X (B)	—	X	—	—	X
ob	X	X	X (B)	—	—	X	—	X
an	X	X	X (K)	X	X	—	—	X
	—	—	X (Ya & Ye)	—	—	—	—	X

rce: Survey IV.
es: Yali camps were at

B	Biliau	N	Nobanob
K	Korog	Ya	Yabob
M	Mukuru	Ye	Yelso

worker by its magic power. But the origin of Elias was lost as
t was passed along from the Rai Coast. In Madang most people
knew only its name and that the 'wind' of Elias as it passed could
seek out sinners, especially adulterers and those who employed
sorcery, and kill them. In some villages houses were built and
stocked with provisions against the prolonged night which Elias
was expected to bring. Eventually Elias was escorted to a water-
hole near Sek associated with two traditional culture heroes,

D

Kilibob and Manup, and there it is said to have disappeared in a thunderclap. Afterwards several of the men who had brought Elias to Sek saw the 'hammer' of Kilibob in a house there.

Tagarab of Mirkuk was an ex-policeman and widely feared for his physical strength and temper. Around 1937 he started a communal market gardening scheme in which several villages near his own cooperated. Produce was sold to contacts he had made in the police force in Madang Town. But this was no ordinary project, because in the garden was a house in which Tagarab had the 'hammer' of the hero, Kilibob, and this as much as the gardening was expected to produce money. At first Tagarab organized his garden at Silabob where he had kinsmen. But later this land was the subject of a dispute between Silabob and Foran so he transferred his 'work' to Panim land on which Mirkuk village also lives. Tagarab then abandoned the garden and concentrated entirely on ritual associated with traditional deities and the sacred relic. The cult came to an end when Tagarab, who had collaborated with the Japanese, joined their retreat to the Sepik. He was later shot by them for treachery.

Between 1939 and about 1946 a cult called Letub (see also Inselmann 1944) appeared in many of the villages. Traditional dances were performed, and both dancers and audience sometimes fell into shaking fits and trances. Ritual varied according to local interests and traditions. Frequently visits were made to the cemeteries and food offered to the dead. Some people had dreams and visions in which dead relatives showed them how they could make money or where they could find it, and rebuked them for their sins. Others foretold the future, found lost items or detected hidden sins. It was said that the dead would not speak to those who had unreconciled quarrels or unconfessed adultery and sorcery. It appears that at the time Letub was something of a reaction against the mission (Inselmann 1944, pp. 114–15, 199) but today several informants say it was the work of the Holy Spirit.

The next important events centred on Yali Singina of Sor village on the Rai Coast, about 50 miles by sea from Madang. His story has been told in great detail by Peter Lawrence (1964) and only the main events will be summarized here. In the period of unrest which followed the Second World War, because of his outstanding war record, Yali was appointed by the District

Officer to put over Australian propaganda to the villages. Yali encouraged villages to combine in large camps which were organized in a clean and orderly fashion. But his scheme was soon reinterpreted in Madang in terms of the local people's search for wealth and the pursuit of cargo. Yali himself gave up attending church services, openly supported the men's cult in his home village (similar but not identical to that in Madang), and soon ceased to repudiate cargo doctrine. In 1950, largely on information provided by hostile Christians, he was gaoled for five years for illegally imprisoning people and incitement to rape. During Yali's period in gaol, overt activities in his name were largely suspended.

In 1944 an individual known in the villages under study as Kaumaip apparently visited the area and started local cult houses which informants described as similar to those organized a little later by Owro. However, none of these villages was involved in the Bagesin rebellion led by Kaumaip in 1944 (Lawrence 1964, pp. 110–15). Each operated only in its own interests on its own land. In 1947 Owro from the Bagesin area started work. Food was offered to local deities and ancestors in special cult houses on sacred land in the forest in order to persuade them to bring money. Owro claimed to be able to communicate vocally with the spirits of trees etc. His ritual depended for its success on the cleanliness and good conduct of the adherents. Members had to wash frequently in the river or in hot water to rid themselves of sin. The cult came to an end when Owro and others were imprisoned.

YALI'S MOVEMENT

Open support for Yali increased after he left gaol in 1955, and especially in the 1960s. During my stay in the area I collected information on the current practices of his movement. Yali is revered and feared for his powers of intercession with pagan deities. He is frequently referred to euphemistically as 'the Old Man' (*lapun* or *lapun papa*) or 'the Big Man of the Rai Coast' (*bikpela bilong Rai Kos*). Many stories are told about miraculous events in his life. It is said that when he was in gaol at Lae a noose was prepared to hang him, but the gallows, made from a local tree, said 'You can't hang him. If you do it will be the end of both blacks and whites.' His followers believe firmly in his sacredness. One village leader told his children he wished to be buried with his picture of Yali. There is loyalty and pride in loyalty to Yali. As one informant put it, 'We don't move to a new village site and then go back to the old one' (we won't go back on Yali).

Yali is called the 'king' of New Guinea by his followers and held responsible for recent developments such as schools, councils, increased wages and the end of prohibition on alcohol for New Guineans. He himself does not claim to be a god or to be able to create money, but in his name, and with the help of sacred bark, magic water and his semen in little bottles, his followers claim to be able to create money and to heal the sick. It is not easy to establish exactly what they expect from him, and he himself is very non-committal. His Delphic statements give room for the enthusiast's imagination to run riot while making it difficult for his enemies to pin him down. Basically followers are waiting for *nupela lo* or *gutpela lo* (the new way of life or the good life). *Lo* is all things to all men. For some it is clearly money, thus, 'We New Guineans have no money. We think Yali will show us the road of money.' For others it is overtly political. One Yali leader described Yali's candidacy in the 1968 House of Assembly elections in the following terms: 'Yali said if they vote me in they'll send me to Port Moresby to open the door of this cult house (*haus tambaran*) and open New Guinea . . . Then a new way of life will come. New Guineans will be leaders. They will wear shirts, trousers and shoes.'

Yali is undisputed head of the cult. Beneath him are the *lo bos* or local leaders in villages where he has followers. Especially where there are only a few supporters, one *lo bos* may cover several villages. They are appointed by Yali on recommendation from other *lo bos*. Literally they are supposed to 'look after' an ill-defined commodity, the *lo*. Their duties involve collecting financial contributions from the faithful, holding meetings in the village and preaching Yali's word. Unmarried girls called flower girls (*meri plaua*) visit Yali once a year and bring away bottles of his semen for ritual use by their fathers and village friends. Yali bases the sexual emphasis of his cult on a letter he is supposed to have received from the sister of a European friend. Apparently the letter revealed that brothels were the source of European wealth. In his home village of Sor, Yali has two very large impressive houses and a household of five wives, children, visiting flower girls, a dozen or so labourers and guests. In his house is Yali's holy room (*rum tambu*) where he keeps cult items and which is if anything can be said to be the physical centre of his whole movement. A stone's throw from his front door is the men's cult house, where he and other Sor villagers celebrate traditional *tambaran* ritual.

But all this is a long way from Madang itself. In the villages here the *lo bos* hold meetings every Tuesday (Yali's official birthday), at which sins are confessed and the latest word from the leader is propounded. *Lo bos* sometimes act as mediators in disputes between supporters of Yali. In fact his followers generally prefer to take their troubles to the *tamaniak* or to an individual mediator rather than to the courts or police.

Certain *lo bos* administer Yali baptisms at $2 a time to wash away Christian baptisms. One *lo bos* told me: 'The mission has soiled people. So we give them a baptism.' The water comes from Sor, and Yali 'puts it right' before the *lo bos* carry it carefully to Madang. One Yali baptism I witnessed took place in the house of the man whose wife was being baptized. The *lo bos* went into a separate room, and stood in silence with his head bowed before a shelf with a jar of leaves on it. When he came back he opened a piece of cloth in which was wrapped a small glass medicine phial. This he cleaned carefully with the cloth. He then brought out another cloth wrapped around a beer bottle containing liquid, from which he poured a little water into the phial. The woman was told to take off her blouse, and sat down in front of the *lo bos*. Slowly he tipped a little water on the hair just in the middle of her head, and rubbed it gently in. Then he dabbed water on each shoulder and between her breasts. The remainder of the water was returned to the phial, and the last remaining drop was tipped onto the woman's head. She rose, put on her blouse and paid $2 to the *lo bos*, who entered her name in an exercise book. The whole ceremony was performed almost in silence before a handful of people, the immediate families of the woman and the *lo bos*, a *lo bos* from another village and the anthropologist. The few instructions which the *lo bos* gave were in Pidgin.

Reference is often made to the Yali rules for behaviour. Unless his followers observe these the good life will remain unattainable. The rules which are publicly acknowledged and repeated concern cleanliness and prohibitions on sorcery, harmful magic,

the beating of wives and dogs, adultery and anger on account o
it. There is however a second layer of meaning. Several Yal
leaders admitted that the prohibition on anger over adultery wa
tok bokis (parable talk) or *tok antap* (a public statement with a
hidden meaning). It did not really mean that you should no
commit adultery but that such an event should not lead to
anger.

A good follower of Yali will not only pay annual taxes to
him, but will also set aside money for him when he sins, and
also every time he cuts down a tree or kills an animal which i.
under the protection of a traditional deity. Yali's income i
difficult to estimate. In actual taxes as opposed to tree and anima
contributions each village should pay a minimum of $10 p.a
On one occasion a *lo bos* visited Yali with contributions o
$2.50, $2.00, $1.00, $1.00, 60¢ and 60¢ from six fellow villagers

Different people sometimes develop their own money-making
ritual in Yali's name, using a table and a jar of leaves and some
object associated with Yali, such as one of his election posters
Husbands and wives or other couples also sometimes *sutin
plaua* (put flowers) i.e. put their sexual fluids in jars of leaves
In sickness and in trouble followers call on the name of Yali
The *lo bos* report the results of these rituals to him.

The *lo bos* in a particular area often convene, and they also
travel to Sor to deliver money, hear news, discuss problems
collect sacred items or for a special occasion such as the announcement of Yali's heir. It should be mentioned here that Yali is an
old man now and that much of the talking, travelling and doing
is in the hands of his right-hand man, Dui of Warai village nea:
Sor. Yali's heir is the infant son of one of his wives. Yali himsel
admits that he is sterile, but the local theory of multiple paternity
enables him to claim partial responsibility for the children borne
by his wives.

It would be wrong to give the impression that all, or indeec
much, of this organization is general knowledge. Little of it is
known or known for certain to outsiders. As one *lo bos* said
'I only see one or two people quietly at my house. We mustn't
do things in too public a fashion.' This secrecy is largely a function
of the hostility which supporters of Yali face from outsiders
(see Chapter 8). It should be appreciated that Yali's support is
extremely far-flung. He must have adherents in upwards of

100 villages – on the Rai Coast, in the Bogadjim, Bagesin, Matu-
gar and Bogia areas as well as Madang. But it is from Madang
supporters that his main financial support comes, and it is with
his Madang supporters that he has the most frequent and enthusiastic contact. Yali himself attributed the support of Madangs
to their long history of cargo cult. He told me, 'The Madangs
follow me because of Letub. So they believed in me. People
without Letub are not interested in me now.'

YAKOB'S CULT

The second cult which I witnessed in the field was that of Yakob
(Jacob). Yakob is an ex-Roman Catholic catechist who ran away
from his job, removing certain church ornaments at the same
time. His story is that he was swimming one day on the reef near
his father's village and swam into a cave. There he met his
ancestors who told him the secret of how to create money.
People paid him a membership fee, and then were allowed to
put red tin or wooden boxes into special houses. The members
were told to perform traditional dances, and to carry the boxes
to sacred spots in the forest and then back again to the cult house.
These efforts did not meet with any noticeable success, and in
February of 1966 an Ambenob Council patrol opened the houses
and boxes and ridiculed the cult.

Only temporarily deterred, Yakob started work again in 1968.
This time he elaborated the ritual, but the boxes were still put
in special houses. Teams of helpers went out to look for money
in pre-arranged spots in the forest. Children found coins, and
older men found false rolls of coins made of wood (purportedly
worth $10) which Yakob said he would later turn into real money.
On one occasion I was present when he performed this magic,
'washing' a single wooden roll and supposedly turning it into
100 real 10¢ pieces. In an inner room the roll was laid on a table
with three 10¢ pieces alongside. Yakob patted water (which had
been magically delivered into a beer bottle) on the roll and the
coins. Then all but he left the room. Outside in the moonlight,
leaders organized chants and handclaps. Then Yakob himself
came outside and sat thoughtfully for 20 minutes or so staring
into space. Then with two or three observers, including myself,
he re-entered the room and revealed the transformation into real
money. At any one time Yakob only produced a very small

number of coins, with the promise of more to come. By continually travelling and explaining the delay in the delivery of money in terms of his followers' hidden resentments and unconfessed sins, Yakob managed to prolong his period of power for almost eight months. Then he went underground to escape the wrath of those he had cheated, and of the police who wanted him for failure to pay for a car he had hired.

The relationship between Yakob's and Yali's cults is complex. Yakob's had flower girls, sexual rituals and jars of leaves. In public Yakob said Yali was 'his father' (i.e. he followed him and was obedient to him). But in private he claimed total responsibility for the activities he supervised. However, it is clear that Yakob's public support for Yali ensured him a large following in Yali strongholds. Yali himself made every attempt to dissociate himself from Yakob.

Initially the Administration actively discouraged cargo activity and punished offenders. The *luluai* of Korog was imprisoned for a month for failing to report the Letub cult, and seven others were also gaoled for taking part in it (Inselmann 1944, p. 116). With Yali, as has already been shown, the policy in the beginning was to use him in propaganda for the Administration. Later however the Administration became suspicious of his intentions. A report of 1950 (D.D.A., Quarterly Report, Madang District, to 30 September 1950. File 29-10-34) reads 'Mr R . . ., in his work of recent months, has done much good work to eradicate the past evil influence of the native, Yali, and there is an appreciable change in the attitude of the native peoples to the Administration.' More recently, however, the Administration in Madang has modified its policy. It is no longer believed that cargo cults could or should be crushed by official opposition. Today officers of the Administration are advised to leave cults strictly alone and to concentrate their efforts on improving social and economic conditions in the affected areas (District Commissioner, personal communication 1969).

The police, however, appear to operate on different lines. While the regular force concerns itself with reported crimes, including those attributed to cargo leaders, Special Branch and detective personnel seem to take a great interest in cargo activities even where no crime has been reported. An official of the Special Branch told me that his department is concerned with the threat of communist cell organization within the framework of cargo cult, while a member of the detective force said it was his job to keep in touch with everything that happens in his area, criminal or not. This policy, whether official or individual, results in a great deal of questioning, visiting and surveillance of cultists. For example many boats which come in from the Rai Coast are met by observers who pride themselves on knowing who is travelling where on Yali's business.

The policy of European missionaries has always been to treat cargo cults as perversions of and/or antagonistic to Christianity and hence to discourage them. Thus missionaries Inselmann and Walck preached and talked against cargo at Nobanob. The Lutheran Mission's official policy was, however, not always clear to its New Guinean workers and officials, who sometimes countenanced if not encouraged cargo cults. Today however Yali's movement is universally condemned by local church workers (see Chapter 8 below).

TWO MODELS FOR THE COMPARATIVE STUDY OF CULTS

This account prepares the ground for later consideration of the political implications of cargo cult, justifies my isolation of Yali's movement as a special case, and underlines those features of this cult which are significant for later discussion. Worsley (1957, p. 228) proposes that cargo cults weld together previously hostile and separate groups in a new unity. When we look at the Madang cults in these terms, it appears that this unifying effect is not identical for them all, and in fact could be treated as a variable in comparative analysis.[1] Simply because a cult appears in more than one village, it should not be assumed that it creates any new ties or that it represents a new form of inter-village activity. It seems possible in this framework to extract models of two different types of cult. On the one hand, there is the small-scale cult, spreading along traditional channels, operating in village units with little institutionalized connection between them and scant formal organization, invoking supernatural powers specific to each village and thus not in competition with Christianity or other cults elsewhere. In contrast to this is the large-scale cult, spreading along non-traditional channels of communication,

[1] Both Lawrence (1964, pp. 235–6) and Worsley (1957, p. 254) hint at this kind of distinction.

with a highly developed inter-village organization and formal internal structure, centralized ritual and universalized doctrines and aims. I shall consider in turn each of the various elements in these models.

There is a great difference in scale between Yali's cult and the others. None of the others affected more than 20 villages, whereas Yali's organization today must cover more than 100. The scale of the cults is linked to the way in which when they were new they spread from village to village. The smaller cults travelled along traditional channels of kinship or other traditional person-to-person relationships. F. E. Williams describes the transmission of the Orokaiva Taro Cult in the same terms (1928, pp. 17–18). These cults seem to have moved from one village to the next only by virtue of some pre-existing personal tie which led to an introduction to the leader or an opportunity to buy the ritual. In Madang, out of 42 cases where we know how a small cult came to a new village, on 36 occasions cults were transmitted through person-to-person relationships, 29 being those created by inter-village marriage (Survey IV). In only six cases did the cult leader arrive in a village on his own initiative. Hence these cults tended to be found in patches corresponding to the clusters of villages between which there were the largest number of inter-personal ties. Some of the early contacts between Yali's Rai Coast supporters and two or three villages on the coast near Madang followed traditional trade ties (Lawrence 1964, p. 35 and Yali himself). The majority of villages however came to see and hear about Yali through his work for the Administration. He became widely known and respected on his patrols along the coast, and in the meetings he held for inland headmen and villagers. When later he became associated with cargo and dissociated from the Administration, it was largely through the camp leaders and contacts he had made during this period that he established communications. We see then that few cargo cults spread by direct proselytization, and in many cases, far from creating new ties between villages, the cults utilized pre-existing inter-village relationships. Nor can it be argued that cargo cults added a new dimension to affinal relations between villages. In traditional times, too, these were exactly the ties used to introduce innovations in *tambaran* ritual and to purchase new dances.

We can also look at the actual activities involved in the cults.

In many of the smaller ones the ritual seems to have been re-created and performed entirely separately in each village. In some cases a few villages combined, as when one or two Kauris and some Korogs joined Opis in an Owro cult house on Opi land. But this type of cooperation is said to have existed in traditional ritual when affines from other villages could join in particular cult celebrations. In Yali's movement too this local ritual element is found, but for the *lo bos* there are also the centralized celebrations at Sor. Because some of them come from other areas, the *lo bos* do not all take an active part in Sor rituals, but they attend, watch, enter the cult house, help with the work and some join in the dancing. Sacred bark, Yali's semen, water for baptisms etc. are all produced centrally at Sor. Yali's organization is widespread, and has a hierarchy of leaders who are in contact over a large area. In the other cults village leaders have little contact with one another, and then only through the cult leader. This contrast is reflected in the fact that the language of communication in Yali's movement is Pidgin, while most of the smaller cults have operated almost entirely in local languages.

Yali's movement can also be contrasted with the smaller cults in terms of its general structure. While the distribution of power within the latter is largely *ad hoc*, in Yali's movement it is institutionalized in a number of offices. Over time the activities of Yali's movement have become regularized and centrally regulated, as those of the smaller cults are not. None of these has lasted more than five years, while Yali's followers have been supporting him, if intermittently, since the 1940s. In this sense Yali's movement can be seen to be taking on aspects of an established religion rather than a typical cargo cult.

Furthermore, particularistic elements were more important in the smaller cults. The supernatural forces they invoked were specific not solely to the leader, but to a considerable extent also to the performers. The legend on which the leader's power was based, the magic stones used in the ritual, or the sacred land where a cult house stood, were the property of particular groups. Neither they nor the benefits derived from them could be freely shared. Yali's cult relies less on locally owned ritual objects and more on the powers of Yali himself, the materials he dispenses, and the ritual he performs at Sor. His followers are united in their dependence on a ritual strength outside their own village.

Similarly, the benefits expected from the smaller cults are restricted to individual paid-up members, while there is a sense in which Yali's movement aims to bring salvation to all black-skinned New Guineans.

Finally, Yali's teachings are held by him and his followers to be incompatible with other views held in Madang. This has not always been the case with the smaller cults in which the ritual and deities were contextually specific and belonged to certain groups. In 1968 another cult very similar to Yakob's was influential in the area immediately to the north of Kamba and Haidurem. Madangs did not see these two cults as rivals to each other. Often, therefore, there is no conception of incompatibility either between different cults or between any of them and Christianity. Yali's cult, on the other hand, exhibits a high degree of intolerance to both pagan (including cargo) and Christian alternatives. In such attitudes there are obvious political advantages for Yali which did not exist for the leaders of more localized cults. In 1968 Yakob was collecting tribute and gaining influence in some of the strongholds of Yali's movement. To win adherents he publicly emphasized his support for Yali and their common interests and techniques. Yali on the other hand did everything he could to discredit Yakob, whom he saw as a rival and interloper. So while Madangs feel that they have to choose between Christianity and Yali, they think that support for either is compatible with following Yakob.

Not only is each of the variables discussed in itself a basis for comparative analysis, but it appears that certain characteristics are clustered and interrelated. Because Yali was not limited to traditional channels of communication his movement was able to spread more widely. Because they were localized in different areas, Yakob and the leader to his north were not in competition. Because Yali's movement spanned many language groups and a wide area, he had to offer a centralized ritual authority to which people of different cultural backgrounds could turn in harmony.

In presenting these two clear-cut types I would not want to argue that any particular cult necessarily fits into either slot. Furthermore it is likely that over time a cult may shift its position on the continuum between the two poles. It seems that this has in fact been the case with Yali's movement. In their early stages his doctrines and those of different groups of his followers probably had more local and particularistic elements than today. Similarly over time the administrative structure of the movement has been elaborated and this in turn has brought new elements of uniformity to the movement as a whole.

There is also considerable ideological and ritual similarity between all the cults which have appeared in Madang. They are all, at least in part, a response to the same widely felt and continuing problem, which one informant eloquently expressed as follows:

The Europeans blocked the road and our parents were still in darkness when they bore us. We were unable to find money. The mission originally came and said: if you work for money you won't believe in God. Who will show us the good road on this earth so that we can see it and understand it? Who will come and show us the road?

In his exposition Peter Lawrence (1964) points out that in response to a new situation and new demands people all over the southern Madang District turned to a common traditional epistemology and ritual heritage. Thus we find similar themes in many cults – reference to the legendary brothers, Kilibob and Manup, appeals to the dead and an emphasis on peace in the community. Sexual rituals and an emphasis on hygiene are other elements common to several cults. Several informants made deliberate attempts to trace continuity between cults. For example one said that in Letub rituals the ghosts of the dead used Yali's name. There has also been considerable continuity of personnel, the same men playing prominent parts in several movements.

For the purposes of this book, however, it is not the similarities between many of the Madang cults, but the differences between Yali's movement and the others which are important. It is the unique features of Yali's movement – its scale, persistence, growth, organization and ritual – which have made it, alone of all the cults, a major political force in Madang and beyond.

PART II
MADANG TODAY

3

The Social Framework

The composition of the basic residential unit has changed considerably from traditional times. Today there are no men's houses or *haus tambaran*, and most men live, sleep and eat with their wives and unmarried children in a single house. On marriage a couple usually occupies a separate house near members of the husband's clan or village. In Kauris today the average size of households is four persons. In no village under study do all members live in a single settlement. The pattern is of a group of hamlets (and occasional isolated homes) dispersed over village land. For example, in Kauris there are five multiple-household hamlets and two single households living in isolation, about half the households being resident on their own clan land. There is considerable clustering by clan, and in many cases the hamlets of one village are clearly closer to one another than to those of other villages. Changes in the pattern of settlement seem attributable largely to the introduction and continuance of dispersive factors (e.g. sorcery, quarrels and cash cropping) and the decrease in factors making large settlements imperative (e.g. traditional warfare and Administration policy in the 1940s). It should be appreciated that the combination of households in hamlets as well as the siting of these settlements varies over time. Members of Bara clan in Kauris, for example, have made eight moves since 1900.

As we have already seen, about 24 per cent of adult male members are absent either in towns or educational institutions. I shall not be concerned with these people to any great extent here. However it should be noted that this is a considerable proportion of the Madang village population and that as such it constitutes an important divergence (e.g. in the day-to-day composition of the village *tamaniak*) from the traditional situation.

E

FOREIGNERS[1] RESIDENT ON VILLAGE LAND

A large number of people resident on village land today are not members of the land-holding clans. Approximately 30 per cent of adult males and 26 per cent of the total population resident on Madang village land are foreigners (Survey I). For descriptive purposes I have divided these people into three categories:

Table 5. Foreigners resident in 13 villages covered by Survey I

Village	'Friends and affines'		Labourers		Residents in discrete settlements		Totals	
	Adult males	Whole popn.	Adult males	Whole popn.	Adult males	Whole popn.	Adult males	Wh. po;
Barahaim	—	—	—	—	—	—	—	—
Foran	10	23	5*	5*	15*	55*	30*	8
Kamba	3	14	7	8	—	—	10	2
Kauris	—	—	13	16	—	—	13	1
Korog	9	32	—	—	—	—	9	3
Mirkuk	—	—	—	—	—	—	—	—
Mis	6	22	5	5	57*	125*	68*	15
Nobanob	7	26	—	—	—	—	7	2
Opi	—	—	—	—	—	—	—	—
Panim	13	50	—	—	—	—	13	5
Silabob	7	22	3	3	—	—	10	2
Urugan	6	15	—	—	—	—	6	1
Yahil	5	22	—	—	—	—	5	2
Totals	66	226	33	37	72*	180*	171*	44

* Estimated.

'friends and affines', labourers, and residents in discrete settlements (see Table 5). The largest number are 'friends and affines'. These people usually live close to their individual hosts but some (especially those who have left home because of quarrels and sorcery fears) choose to live by themselves. About half the population of Mirkuk village lives on Panim land as a result of a

[1] The term 'foreigner' is used in this book for New Guineans who are not resident in their own villages. 'Expatriate' refers to a non-New Guinean. In addition to the foreigners detailed in this section, there were also seven expatriates resident on Madang village land; one of the four adult males ran a store and tavern near his house, while the other three worked in and around town.

war in pre-contact times, but this is ignored in the present discussion. Of the 66 males in Table 5, 17 originally came from others of the villages under study. Most of the other migrants are from places relatively close at hand, 41 out of the total 66 coming from within the Madang Sub-District.

The reasons why these 'friends and affines' have come to live in Madang are various. A considerable proportion of the cases (23 out of 66) represent the cumulative effect of migration; they are either the children of earlier migrants or have moved into the area to join relatives who had previously migrated there. The importance of the proximity of Madang Town is also evident. In 25 cases the migrants originally came to the area to find employment. Informal contacts at work, the market or religious and social gatherings were the basis of friendships which eventually led to their move from town to village. Fear of sorcery and quarrels are further reasons for migration, especially between neighbouring villages. As one Mirkuk informant told me, 'A lot of young children died [from sorcery], so I went to Yahil'. In 38 of the 62 cases for which I recorded the information migrants were residing with their affines. It should not be assumed that such men had affinal ties in a village before they came there; in several cases migrants have married after their arrival. For instance, one man from about 20 miles away in the Madang Sub-District worked with a Madang man at the General Hospital. He was invited to save money on accommodation by living with his friend in his home village and later married this man's sister. But those who have moved on account of disputes are likely to seek refuge with pre-existing affines.

Foreign labourers account for only about 5 per cent of all adult males living on Madang village land. Unlike the last category of foreigners discussed, few of these are accompanied by families. Villagers employ labourers to work on their coconut and cocoa plantations, though only the most successful of farmers can afford this kind of assistance. Because there are virtually no sources of cash income in their remote home areas, these labourers are prepared to work for the very low wages offered by their Madang employers. Several receive only $36 p.a. plus access to land for gardens and occasional extra gifts. Sometimes they are also able to sell garden produce at Madang market. Those from Wanuma, about 40 miles north-west of Madang

Town, made their original contact with Madang villagers through a Kauris Lutheran who was a mission teacher on Wanuma Station from 1960 to 1965. Some labourers live with or near their employers, but those who are part of a fairly large labour force have separate accommodation.

The third category of foreigners in Madang live in separate settlements and have the least social contact with the land-owners. The proximity of Madang Town has made two of the villages, Foran and Mis, attractive to people from farther away (Rai Coast, Sepik and the trans-Gogol, for example) who want to work in town or grow and sell garden produce there. Living on village land can reduce the cost of housing and food for workers as well as augmenting their income. For such reasons several discrete settlements of foreigners have grown up in the two villages mentioned. Some residents of these settlements are employed irregularly, if at all, and the sale of garden produce in Madang market is their main source of income. The original settlers have usually made contact with the particular villager on whose land they live. In 1963, for example, two men from the Tapen area of the Rai Coast came to Matupi Plantation looking for work. There was none available, and they were rescued from their predicament by a member of the Sagalau Primary 'T' School Parents and Citizens' Committee, who gave them work on the school grounds. When the P. and C. found this too expensive the two Tapens asked their Mis benefactor to lend them land to plant sweet potatoes for sale. Today there are about 40 Tapens in the settlement, and they sometimes help their host to plant coconuts. This example shows that the line between such foreigners and labourers is rather arbitrary.

PERSONS RESIDENT ON ALIENATED LAND WITHIN TRADITIONAL VILLAGE TERRITORY

Expatriate and New Guinean mission workers, teachers, prison officials and plantation personnel live on alienated land close to (and in some cases among) Madang villagers. No adequate official census had been made of these people by the time I left the field, and their minor significance for village politics did not seem to justify my conducting my own. As a rough guide, however, in the whole Ambenob Multi-Racial Council area 13 per cent of the total population and 19 per cent of males over 18 years are registered as resident on alienated land (D.D.A., letter of 20/11/69 appended to Patrol Report 6 of 1969/70, Madang District). I would estimate that around 350 adult males are resident on land alienated from the Madang villages (excluding those resident on areas now included within the town boundary).

MARRIAGE

Marriage is important not only as an area of interaction *per se* but also because of its significance for other areas of interaction in which individuals, some of whom are linked by ties of marriage, participate. The main departure from traditional practice has been the introduction of courtship in which one or both partners makes the initial move. Many such marriages are socially accept-able despite the departure from traditional usage and in fact marriages made in this way account for 54 per cent of all those in which sample members have been involved (Survey I). The proportion of courtship marriages is increasing. The burden of accepting or rejecting, or even initiating, a marriage proposal frequently rests on the woman and her family. After a marriage has been concluded there is still an imbalance between wife-givers and wife-receivers which is recognized, for example, by the obligation to pay brideprice. Sometimes there is also a small reciprocal presentation of pots and pans to the bride. Contribu-tions to the brideprice come mainly from the husband himself, his nuclear family and his clan, but in some cases also from his mother's clan and his sister's husband. The cash, pigs, plates, clay pots, traditional valuables and garden food which make it up are always handed over to the woman's nuclear family, in particular her father. A part may later be redistributed, especially to her mother's natal clan. The assembly and distribution of brideprice is not only an opportunity for the expression of solidarity between clansmen and kinsmen, it is also an occasion for ambitious men to display their resources, express an interest in certain individuals and incur their gratitude. A clan's informal leader may make a contribution disproportionate to the closeness of his tie with the groom as a statement and enhancement of his position. In one distribution, for example, when a dispute arose between the bride's adopting and natal fathers over claims to the brideprice, it was handed over to a prominent village councillor. But a man's obligation to his wife's family is a continuing one, the fulfilment of which can enhance his prestige and call forth reciprocal presentations and assistance from his in-laws. One informant told me that when he married 20 years ago he was younger than his wife and her relatives taunted him: 'You are too young and will not be able to pay for her. We shall never eat any pigs.' It is a source of pride to him when he calculates that over the years of his marriage he has presented his wife's family with 32 pigs in all. This man is an exceptionally energetic and successful participant in traditional spheres of exchange. Few men would rise to these heights.

A man's children are in constant danger from the *wetu* (Kamba) or angry spirit of their mother's brother and/or his children. *Wetu* is not regularly invoked in a curse or spell; it is the automatic result of anger following the blood (and only the blood) relationship between a man and his sister's children. If a man is angry with his sister's husband it is the children who are expected to suffer. Thus an informant said of his brother-in-law, 'I gave him pigs when he asked, in case he was cross and my child was sick.' The effect of this, the most powerful road of *wetu*, is different from that of other people's *wetu*. The anger of a father or father's brother will only cause sickness, while that of the mother's brother is believed also to make a man abandon his gardens, neglect house building, fail to marry or become aimlessly promiscuous. It is believed to make women barren. In order to avoid such a fate for his children a man gives valuables, services, pigs, money and food to his wife's brother. Sometimes he may send a gift as a general insurance policy 'in the name of' one of his children. The wife's brother has no reciprocal obligation of this kind, but in turn makes pacificatory payments to his own wife's brother. Thus, while the marriage itself puts a man in debt to his wife's father, the bearing of children puts him at a disadvantage with his wife's brother. For at least two further generations the descendants of a couple are involved in a modified form of this relationship.

THE DISTRIBUTION OF MARRIAGES

Only a very small proportion of marriages (4 per cent) are made within the clan (Survey III). The main restriction on such marriages is the prohibition on marriage within three generations of blood kin on either side. The number of permitted spouses within the clan who are also single and of an appropriate age is another restricting factor. Informants also said in reference to brideprice: 'We don't want to eat our own pigs', implying that it was preferable for wife-givers and wife-receivers to be in different clans. It can also be argued that there is little advantage in making an affine of a clansman with whom one already has many reciprocal obligations. Such intra-clan marriages as are recorded are found in exceptionally large clans, clans which include several distinct lineages (e.g. Nobanob Hibutba), and where at least one party has been adopted into the clan.

Forty-eight per cent of all marriages are made within the village (Survey III). Considering that earlier marriages have resulted in bringing fellow villagers within the prohibited degrees, and that the number of single men and women available at any one time is limited, this high proportion seems to indicate a significant preference for intra-village marriage. The argument is borne out by the fact that in the five largest villages, where these limiting factors are least likely to operate, the proportion of intra-village marriage is roughly twice that in the five smallest. There are a number of reasons for favouring intra-village marriage. The high degree of social contact between fellow villagers facilitates courtship or arrangement of marriages. In addition many of the advantages of affinal relationships (particularly those perceived by the woman and her kin) are increased the closer to one another the affines live. A shortage of women (47 to every 53 men) also inclines people, so informants told me, to distribute this scarce resource among their fellow villagers rather than assisting others further afield. Once established, and within the limits of the prohibited degrees, a pattern of intra-village marriage appears to be self-perpetuating (as indeed does any pattern), because there is a feeling that a woman should be returned if not in one's own then at least in a subsequent generation. Bridewealth is inadequate to wipe out this indebtedness. The advantages of marriage beyond the village are access to trade, credit, labour and specialized resources, but these appear mainly to be appreciated by men ambitious for prestige and leadership (see Chapter 7 below).

All this means that within the village there is a high density of person-to-person ties. The obligations to a neighbour for his own sake may be limited, but obligations to him as wife's brother or mother's brother's son are numerous. Not only is the average man likely to have more such ties within his own village than with any other single village, but affinal ties within the village are likely to have more practical content.

In Madang 52 per cent of all marriages are made outside the home village (see Appendix II, Table 22, figures relating only to landowners). Although up to now no Madang man has married a European or Asiatic, there has been a fairly large number of marriages between people of different administrative districts (6 per cent of all Madang wives). There has also been a smaller number (3 per cent) with women from areas within the Madang District but more than nine miles from their husband's village, e.g. from the Rai Coast, Bogia, Bunabun and Bundi areas. Such marriages are clearly a departure from traditional patterns and, because of the distances involved, imply a considerable reduction in the level of interaction between affines. It is consonant with the minimal social contact between the two groups that there have been no marriages with labourers and few, if any, with the discrete settlements of foreigners. As indicated already, there has been a certain amount of marriage with other migrants to the area.

From the data collected in Survey I, I have been able to show certain patterns in the inter-village marriages contracted within the District. For statistical purposes, this analysis is limited to the 42 per cent of all marriages between inhabitants of villages less than nine miles apart. Full details of the analysis, including tables, are set out in Appendix II. It appears that language, distance and whether or not the partners' villages own adjacent territory are all significant variables. Marriages are most frequent between villages with adjacent territory. The variable of second importance is distance; villages within three miles of each other are more likely to intermarry than those within six or nine miles. Absolute distance is secondary therefore to the relative position of villages. The variable which rates third in order of importance is language, marriage being most likely between villages speaking the same language. The greatest likelihood of marriage occurs when these three variables coincide, i.e. between villages which are within three miles of each other, share a common language and have adjacent territory. The direction of previous marriages is probably also an important influence.

It also appears from the data that many villages have a tendency to find their spouses predominantly in some one other village. Thus Barahaim-Korog, Haidurem-Mukuru and Kauris-Kamba form pairs. In each of these about or a little below one-third of all extra-village marriages are with the other village of the pair. Thus we see a concentration of extra-village marriages in a single direction (a factor which may also have considerable political significance for the networks within each pair). There is also some directional bunching of extra-village marriages for seven of the other villages, such that at least one-fifth and some-times as much as one-half of such marriages are with one other. Differences in the proportions of extra-village marriages (varying from 100 per cent to 13 per cent) and in their distribution result in very different individual patterns for the different villages. Nobanob, with 87 per cent of wives coming from within the village, only has women from four local villages, while Foran, a much smaller village, has women from 10 others. Opi has yet another pattern. All its wives come from outside, but it draws on only four villages and receives one-half and one-third respec-tively from Korog and Gal. Such patterns can be related to the desire to perpetuate affinal links through the generations.

THE SPECTRUM OF SOCIAL RELATIONSHIPS

The political and economic content of particular relationships will be discussed in later chapters. Here I am concerned to identify the various categories of people with which an individual has what might be called, rather residually, social contact. The corporate group to which the individual appears to turn most commonly for assistance is his clan. For example, adoption appears to be relatively common in Madang, involving, by their own account, at least 38 per cent of sample members (Survey I). Of these adoptions, 45 per cent were made within the clan, many of these being the adoption of children by their fathers' brothers. It appears that more boys than girls are adopted within the clan. Although sons and daughters have the primary responsibility for the care of sick and aged parents, it seems that the clan is regarded as having residual obligations in this respect. One widow in Kauris (with two married daughters living elsewhere) was under the wing of her husband's clan brother, his actual FaFaFaBro-SoSoSo. This man built her a house near his own, distributed a compensation payment on her behalf after a dispute involving her daughter and allowed her to use his cocoa cooperative members' number to earn the higher members' price for wet beans. The cocoa she sold was planted for her by a FaFaBroSoSo of her husband, i.e. another member of his clan. Certain feasts and food payments are also organized on clan (and ultimately village) lines. In one case members of another village made a compensatory payment to Kauris after a dispute over the marriage of a Kauris girl to one of their own men. The payment was distributed among Kauris people by the girl's widowed mother's protector (see above). He divided the garden food into five equal parts, subsuming two clans under their respective senior clans and disregarding the numerical strength of each clan and distributed other items slightly in favour of his own clan.

It has already been suggested in this chapter that the village contains the greatest density of affinal and cognatic ties. Partly as a result of this, many other kinds of cooperative links are concentrated within it. For instance, 77 per cent of all adoptions are made within the village (45 per cent, as already mentioned, being within single clans). Fellow villagers also enjoy many informal social contacts, visits, baby-sitting, talking, shared meals, etc. One of the few formal social activities at the village level is traditional-style dancing. One man owns the dance and, supported by his clan, organizes and leads performances. In a village where there is much division on other issues, a series of rehearsals for a traditional dance provides one of the main opportunities for villagers to cooperate happily together. As a body they take the dance to another village to honour someone there or where someone wants to buy it. As a body they compete with other villages at large parties to see who is the best turned out, the best rehearsed and the most attractive to women. As a modern extension of this, many villages have their own guitar groups among their younger men. These practise together and have a group of supporters from their own village who always dance to their group when they go to big parties. Such groups are known locally by their village names, for example the 'Mis team' or the 'Panim team', and even some of the older men take an interest and pride in the successes of their own guitar group.

In addition to his group membership, every individual has a constellation of non-agnatic cognates and affines with whom he may enjoy many kinds of cooperation above and beyond those specific to the relationships concerned. He may wish to benefit from services not available in his own village – sorcery, hired assassination, divination or healing; he may wish to employ a skilled craftsman or builder or buy magic or a dance. Through the mediation of a contact such as his wife's brother in another village, he can gain access to the desired goods or services. He can turn to his affines and other relatives for hospitality when he is travelling, for accommodation if he comes from a remote area and is working in town, and to allow his children or his wife to sleep in their home while they are attending school or receiving treatment at a medical aid post in their village. Affines and non-agnatic cognates also figure prominently among those who turn out to help other villages perform dances or prepare feasts. At a dance rehearsal I attended at Silabob in May 1968 there were 17 affines of various kinds from other villages, six of them performing and the remainder providing the all-important audience.

While cognatic relationships are ascriptive, the degree to which these and affinal relationships are activated varies with the temperament, the geographical location and the interests of the parties concerned. Many adult men do not have relatives of all the possible categories. For example, 64 per cent have no true living adult mother's brother at all (Survey II). Since many aspects of this relationship derive from the 'blood' tie, they are not involved in behaviour towards classificatory mothers' brothers.

A number of person-to-person ties are independent or partly independent of affinal and cognatic links. Certain trading partnerships have survived from traditional times, and newer ones have been established in the traditional style. There is also a new form of friendship with the man known in Pidgin as *wanwok*, the man who works or worked with you. As villagers have travelled to many parts of Papua New Guinea they have struck up acquaintances with co-workers. Such relationships have most practical significance, however, when they are made with fellow workers in Madang Town. Then *wanwok* may be invited home for the weekend, may assist with loans and may provide companionship particularly in social situations in town. Several people have also developed friendships with school or college mates from other villages and areas. Relationships between council, church and cult officials will be discussed in later chapters. Some villagers have developed friendships with people they have met on visits to the District Office, commercial concerns or hospitals. One Kauris woman was in hospital for several weeks and her husband, while living there and looking after her, met two youths from Karkar Island who were also looking after a sick person. The youths had been unable to complete their primary schooling on Karkar, so their new friend invited them to live with him in Kauris and attend Barahaim school; this they did. A few friendships have also sprung up between Madangs and expatriates. One or two of these have led to expatriates building homes on village land (see p. 54 footnote 1).

The Madang attitude to the labourers and foreigners in discrete settlements forms a striking contrast to that in the relationships so far described. Although some Madangs are tolerant, many are quick to point out differences in custom between themselves and the foreigners and to regard them as inferior. I heard it said of one group of labourers that they were stupid and that the various diseases from which they visibly suffered were attributable to their poor diet and hygiene. In not a few instances foreigners are discouraged from mixing socially with the villagers. On one occasion I was present when a group of labourers was sent away from watching a dance rehearsal. Later this action was repudiated by several senior village members, but it nevertheless indicated how some people felt. Other foreigners have minimal social contact with the Madangs for other reasons. The settlement of trans-Gogol people on Mis land is feared by its neighbours because of the powerful sorcery its members are believed to possess. Furthermore although such a settlement may have been initiated through a friendship between a landowner and the man who came there first, later comers may not even know who the landowner is. Sometimes there is friction between foreigners and landowners over the expansion of the settlement or over the use of rivers or trees. Between the landowner and other members of his clan and village there is sometimes disagreement about the admission of the settlers in the first place and this can lead to continuing friction.

Those living on alienated land have, if it is possible, even less social contact with Madang villagers. Plantation, prison and school workers tend to keep themselves to themselves except when, as is true of a few mission teachers, they come from Madang.

Reasons for this are the lack of common economic or political interests, cultural differences, diffidence and the fact that few of any institutions are simultaneously a focus of action for landowners and foreigners (see later chapters on council, cult and church).

4

Economic Activities

The main contrast between the traditional Madang economy and that of today is that the village sphere is no longer autonomous but is related to towns, to plantations, to commercial enterprises operating on Western lines and to extra-village, and in many cases international suppliers and buyers. In these respects it parallels those of peasant systems as they have been described by various writers (for a survey of these see Foster 1967, pp. 2–14). Wage-earners mainly live and work away from home, but some commute daily to jobs in town. From Barahaim, Mirkuk and Panim men work in teams under village foremen as casual stevedores, the number employed depending on the amount of shipping and the standing of a particular village with its employers. As mentioned in Chapter 2, wage labourers have the opportunity to join the Madang Workers' Association. Working for cash is an activity which has no roots in the past, in traditional property or authority relations. Except in the case of stevedoring, the decision to work, the choice of occupation and the finding of employment are the responsibility of the individual. Nevertheless, men who have found work, particularly unskilled work, can introduce fellow villagers to their employer and thus help them find employment. Influential men in the villages can sometimes exercise patronage. The Ambenob councillor responsible for public works was able to secure the job of council road foreman for his eldest son. In this way employment in the extra-village sphere can have implications for the establishment of personal influence and for the performance of officials within that sphere.

Village-based production is both for subsistence and for exchange. There are a number of spheres of exchange. Labour is exchanged for labour, for food and for building materials within the network of kinship and affinity. There are also specific 'valuables', such as dogs' teeth headbands, used in major payments like brideprice. Pigs also are appropriate in brideprice, as in end-of-hostility presentations and payment for specialist services. 'Valuables' and pigs were always individually owned, and it is into the sector of private ownership that cash has moved. This represents a considerable change in favour of the individual in the balance between communally and privately owned assets. It is through cash incomes that villagers feel the effect of external economic influences beyond their control – wage levels in the labour market and world prices for produce. Cash has also become an indispensable part of many traditional-type presentations. It has become increasingly important in brideprice, having been used in 14 out of 15 payments made in the last decade, while only very small amounts of cash were included in 4 out of 20 cases before 1939 (Survey I). Cash also plays a part in presentations designed to harmonize relationships. In one case a bachelor had arranged with some of his friends for a girl in another village to run away to him one night. The couple were fond of each other, but the girl's relatives did not approve of the match. A few days later groups of men from the two villages fought over the girl. In peacemaking discussions, it was agreed that the girl might marry her lover, but that he must pay her clan for his breach of good relationships. The payment was made three years later, in 1968, and was not brideprice. It consisted of a cow purchased for $60, two cartons of beer, five string bags of garden food, 4 lb. sugar, ½ lb. tea, four loaves of bread and six branches of areca nut. The husband who assembled this payment was the highest-paid member of his village, earning between $12 and $16 p.w. as a grader driver.

Today, as in the past, individuals make decisions about the type and extent of the production in which they engage. The introduction of steel axes has made possible more extensive cultivation, and guns have seriously depleted wild pigs in the forest, but there are still some families which rely more heavily than others on hunting and gathering. Each individual also chooses in cooperation with his household whether and how he will try to earn cash. He may choose wage labour, trucking, a trade store, market gardening, selling cattle or pigs or growing one of the introduced commercial crops such as cocoa.

As the population has risen, cash crops have been introduced and many hundreds of acres of land have been alienated, land has become more scarce and desirable than it always was. Today there is probably more variation in land values than in the past because of the soil and terrain requirements of particular cash crops, varying proximity to town and differential access to roads. Madangs obtain rights to land in a number of different ways. The ultimate ownership and control of most land lies with the clan, and the use of a considerable proportion of it is still decided regularly by clan *tamaniak*. But there appears to be some conflict between collective control of land and individual production of cash crops. In the traditional land allocation system the clan re-considered the distribution of land every year, but tree crops grow and bear fruit over a number of years. An example of this and a number of associated problems can be given here.

Case 1. A coconut planter operating on another clan's land

K. of B. clan planted coconuts for commercial purposes on the land of another clan, L., in his village. Today K. says he had the permission of a senior L. member to do this. This man is now dead, and his two clan sons disagree over K.'s occupation of their land. One has no objection, but the other argues that the old man gave K. permission without consulting the L. clan *tamaniak*, so that his decision is not binding on other members. This brother says K. must leave the land because it is not his. K. replies that he has invested $900 in the plantation in labour and tools, and has offered either to surrender the land on payment of this sum in compensation for improvements or to buy it outright for $80. The deadlock had not been resolved when I left the field.

To give more security of tenure to those investing in cocoa and coconuts, clan *tamaniak* have begun to divide some but never all of their land among their members. Bara clan in Kauris, for example, allocated only 12 of its 18 named land sections. The portions left under communal control allow a certain amount of flexibility for the future. The individual recipients have usufructory rights and may transmit the land and crops to a son or sons. Usually these new rights are legally recognized only in cases of dispute, or where the plantation owner is applying for a loan from the Development Bank.

Rightholders still give gardening space to non-agnatic kin and affines. Sometimes a man invites such people to help him clear an area of forest and then allocates to them a portion of the cleared land. In other situations a landowner may recommend to his clan *tamaniak* that a kinsman be allocated an area to clear for himself. On average about 50 per cent of men have one garden on the land of non-agnatic kin or affines (Survey I). A considerable number of people may have gardens in an area nominally cultivated by one man. For example, one man in his mid-50s was the major occupant of land on which he himself, his son and daughter-in-law, his married daughter, his WiMoFa-BroSo, a clan daughter and a clan son, all had gardens. Outsiders to the clan are much more readily admitted as subsistence or part-subsistence farmers than as wholly commercial cultivators. In only 5 per cent of cases is land made available for wholly commercial purposes to non-agnatic kin or affines. The reason seems to be that cocoa and copra require a longer period of occupancy. In addition there is a feeling that a man should not make money out of someone else's land. The sort of problem which can arise when a man plants tree crops on another clan's land has already been illustrated (Case 1).

Access to different types and areas of land may also be obtained by sale or gift, such dealings being particularly likely between men related by marriage. They are only practicable between villages if the land is on the boundary. B. in one village had plenty of good land with road frontage and was the only adult male in his clan. His sister's husband, J., in the next village, was short of such land. J. had always been particularly liberal to B., so B. made J. a gift of a piece of land on the border between their two villages. This was an outright gift and the land is now registered with J.'s clan. One could not say in so many words that J. paid for the land. His extreme generosity to B. continues, but he has not presented him with anything as a price and does not intend to. The Ambenob Cocoa Project is a further source of land for cash croppers (see Chapter 2), and it is interesting to note that this scheme gives foreigners in Madang some security of tenure should they want to plant cocoa. Two foreigners, one on the Opi and one on the Silabob Block, have in fact taken advantage of this provision. The general result of this variety of ways of obtaining land is that at any one time a few men have an area of land under cultivation very much above the average.

A man rarely relies for labour solely on himself and his nuclear family. This does sometimes occur, however, as with one rather anti-social fellow who has long ago exhausted the patience of his

F

kinsmen and his own social credit, or after a bad quarrel when a man 'goes it alone' for a time. More usually Madangs look for assistance when clearing a garden area or starting a new coconut plantation. Frequently a man's clan will turn out for him, sometimes as the result of a formalized arrangement. Such an agreement was made at a meeting of one Kauris clan on 30 June 1968. The *tamaniak* decided to provide a work team for each adult male clan member in turn to clear an area of forest for commercial development. The normal practice is for the garden or plantation owner to provide food for his helpers, and also for

Table 6. Persons assisting K. to cut down forest

	Males	*Females*
1. Own clan	5	—
2. Own affines and other kinsmen: (all from K.'s own village) WiBro another WiBroWi WiBroDa 2× BroWiFaBroSo (one of these being the village *komiti*) Fa2ndWiSo (of a different clan) Fa2ndWiSoWi	4	3
3. Own hired labourers and wife of one of them	5	1
Totals	14	4

their assistance to be entered in the mental ledger of debts and credits in particular relationships. Cooperation between clansmen may lead to joint ownership of assets. Five men in one clan (and other clansmen could have joined if they were interested) worked to enclose a large area near their hamlet in which to keep pigs. The enclosure fence is maintained jointly, but each man has his own hut near the fence where he feeds his own pigs and stores food for them. The single fully grown uncastrated boar is a captured wild one and is jointly owned. All other pigs are the property of individuals.

Other sources of labour are non-agnatic kinsmen and affines, who are rewarded with food and in kind, and hired labourers, the latter mainly for cash crops. Truck drivers and store assistants are sometimes also paid in cash. For any particular project a Madang may utilize labour from a number of sources. His ability to command unpaid assistance is related to his prestige and influence as well as to his capacity to reciprocate. An example can be given from the experience of K., the coconut planter in Case 1. On 7 August 1968, 18 people (see Table 6) turned out to help him cut down an area of forest. This team was partially rewarded by food prepared by K.'s wife, his brother and his wife and another clan brother and his wife.

Although a man can call on clansmen and affines for major projects, for the day-to-day maintenance of gardens and plantations he can only command the assistance of his nuclear family and hired labourers. When a project is likely to yield a large cash profit, there is often a feeling that free labour assistance is inappropriate. This is particularly so when the cash return is immediate. In a commercial dance and party (with entrance fees and food on sale) one man paid all his helpers, even his FaBroDaSo, a relationship in this case very similar to that of SisSo.

Since cash incomes are low and opportunities to save few, Madangs often have to resort to credit to make large payments such as brideprice, for a truck or for wire to fence cattle pasture. From kinsmen and friends a man can get credit on a variety of terms. Sometimes he may not even be expected to repay, e.g. in asymmetrical affinal relationships. Such relationships are an important source of influence for ambitious men (see Chapter 7). A more socially neutral source of credit is the Development Bank.

A considerable quantity of produce is distributed in the non-monetary sphere, goods exchanged for like and unlike goods, between trading partners, affines and other relatives in distant villages as well as between close kinsmen. Some inland villagers have friends in the coastal pot-making village of Yabob and exchange taro for pots, often on Saturdays at the regular market in Madang Town. There is also much distribution in the cash sphere. Vegetables and other garden produce are sold in Madang market, and this activity is the occasion for a certain amount of cooperation at the village level. Many villages charter trucks to go to the market, and once there sellers seat themselves in the same place every week, always with their fellow villagers. Other cash crops are sold to commercial companies, NAMASU, the Copra Marketing Board, the Department of Agriculture and

Madang Cocoa Cooperative. A man can dispose of his income in many ways. He can save his money in a bank account or in his home; he can invest in a cooperative, in major companies, in a trade store or some other commercial enterprise owned by himself; he can lend or give money to relatives and friends (social investment, if you like); he can buy books and uniforms for his children at school and pay their fees; he can contribute to his church or cargo cult, and is legally obliged to pay council tax; he can pay for medicine and medical care; he can buy food, clothing and household goods, such as lamps, alcohol and tobacco, or more expensive items such as a bicycle, a radio, furniture or permanent housing materials.

THE CONSEQUENCES OF CHOICE

The combined range of economic choices (in terms of production, labour, capital, distribution and consumption and investment patterns) has made possible within Madang considerable differentiation in participation in the cash economy, in the control of cash and cash-producing resources and hence in life-styles. A man who makes maximum use of the land available to him, invests and spends his money in appropriate ways, commands credit and a large labour force and himself works with energy and imagination may eventually find himself with an income many times that of the average villager. This study is primarily concerned with politics and I do not claim to have exhaustive or conclusive data on the distribution of incomes in Madang. Rather I present one or two possible indices without suggesting any precise relationship between my figures and the actual distribution of incomes. First, on the assumption that cash cropping is one of the main determinants of different levels of income, I present in Table 7 figures on the ownership of the two major tree crops in the area. Although the figures for individual holdings may not be entirely accurate, the general distribution of trees and palms shows how wide is the gap between the largest growers on the one hand and the majority of the population on the other. Of the 500 or so men who do not own tree crops, some are in paid employment and others are still young and/or undergoing full-time education. Another index of income differences might be variations in savings, although I have no measure of the exact relationship between income and savings. Three-quarters of the adult men own no shares of any kind, even in the cooperative. Table 8 shows that while somewhere around half the men have no bank savings, a small proportion have managed to accumulate

Table 7. Ownership of cocoa trees and coconut palms among Madang men resident in their own Sub-District

| | Number of trees or palms | | | | | | |
	none	1–200	201–400	401–600	601–800	801–1,000	1,000+
of cocoa growers	516	36	57	46	19	7	7
percentage of total population	75	5	8	7	3	1	1
of coconut farmers	511	92	26	7	3	—	4
percentage of total population	79	14	4	1	0·5	—	0·5

Sources: D.A.S.F., Project Areas 6 and 7 (files on individual cocoa and coconut holdings). For 34 of the cocoa growers (not mentioned in the above source) I took earlier and probably somewhat higher figures from D.A.S.F., File 'Councillor Kaut. Agricultural Committee'.

Notes: No figures were available for cocoa holdings in Mukuru or coconut holdings in Foran, Opi or Urugan.

Table 8. Ownership of bank pass books (low-interest-bearing accounts)

Passbooks of informant, wife or dependants	No. of sample members	Percentage of sample
None owned	42	45
Contained up to $5.00	12	13
Contained $5.00 and up to $25.00	16	17
Contained $25.00 and up to $50.00	5	5
Contained $50.00+	9	10
Not known	10	11
	—	—
Total	94	

Note: In nearly all cases pass books were inspected.

what by Madang standards are very considerable sums of money (all data from Survey II).

Although villages away from the road such as Opi and Urugan are on average poorer, there are also considerable economic differences within villages, within clans and even within sibling groups. To illustrate these differences between rich and poor I describe briefly two men who are both members of the same village and have access to similar amenities, roads and types of land. The wealthy man, A., has 2,814 cocoa trees, 1,784 coconut palms and employs between 5 and 10 hired labourers to look after them. He has $900 in the bank, $200 in compound debenture stock in an Australian company, $80 (i.e. 40 Ordinary shares) in NAMASU and shares in the cocoa cooperative. His house is built of sawn timber, fibrolite and roofing iron. His bed has two mattresses, and he usually boils water on a primus stove. He has a table, two forms and two chairs on his central verandah. He owns a large number of tools, household utensils and clothes. He eats meat or fish daily, usually drinks tea in the mornings and smokes about 10 Gold Leaf a day. These items often come from his own small trade store. A. is at pains to appear generous with his clansmen and other supporters, and has made several large and very public loans and presentations. It is my impression, however, that he does refuse many requests for help mainly on the ground that he does not have the ready cash. He is assisted in this by the secrecy which surrounds his financial affairs, and by his investment in a bank account and shares. In contrast to A., B. has no pass book, no shares and apparently little cash in the house. He owns 412 cocoa trees, has no coconuts and no hired labour. His house is made of bush materials, and contains one table and one large bed made entirely of wood. His regular diet includes nothing acquired with cash. He and his family have at the most one change of clothes each and a few household utensils purchased from the stores. B. appears to spend a certain amount on alcohol.

So far in Madang there are no clearly established classes in the Marxist sense of 'differing relations of individuals to the privately owned instruments of production' (Bottomore 1965, p. 19). The Marxist model can of course be applied much more successfully to expatriate-indigenous relationships in Madang Town (see Stevenson 1968, pp. 133–5). Rather the picture is of a large number of independent businessmen operating one-man or one-family enterprises. Only a handful are employers of paid labour. In the more general sense of differences in income and life styles, however, classes can perhaps already be seen. Whether there are elements of discontinuity in political action (as well as an economic and social continuum from rich to poor) is a question which will be considered in Chapters 6 and 8. Today these economic differences are not inherited. All prosperous middle-aged men are self-made. They may have been supported or advised by the senior generation, but they would not have inherited any capital or major tree-crop holdings. For the next generation things may be different, but with large families, equal partition of property among heirs and continuing opportunities for betterment, the situation is likely to remain flexible for some time to come.

POLITICAL ASPECTS OF THREE LOCAL ORGANIZATIONS

All workers in town are eligible for membership of the *Madang Workers' Association* (M.W.A.). Neither in 1968 nor 1969, however, were there any members from the Madang villages in the Stevedores Branch, and in 1969, out of a total membership of 285, only four Nobanob men were members of the Lutheran Mission and Tobacco Factory Branches (Madang Workers' Association, Register of Members). It appears that the M.W.A. has rarely had much support from the inland villages. The Stevedores Branch in particular is dominated by men from Biliau, Kranket, Riwo and Yabob. The leadership of this branch has also rested with the coastal villages for some time; it is a position of considerable potential for an ambitious man. Angmai Bilas, M.H.A. for Mabuso Open electorate, held the chairmanship of this branch as one of his earlier positions. The lack of support for the M.W.A. in the Madang villages stems I think from the very irregular nature of their stevedoring activities (sometimes a village may not work for months), the physical difficulties of attending meetings in town and the small proportion of villagers who work in town; in all these respects they contrast markedly with their coastal neighbours.

The adult male members of the clan in council are recognized by the *Land Titles Commission* (L.T.C.) as the ultimate owners of land. Owing to the continuing and ever increasing importance of land, the clan has retained this, one of its most important traditional functions, and disputes over land are important in many political situations today. An absent member is still theoretically part of this body corporate, and must be consulted about any permanent alienation. Thus a Commission hearing in Kauris was adjourned in September 1969 until the opinions of clan members resident in Lae could be known. Even when members are absent into a second generation, as in Case 2 below, they still retain land rights.

Case 2. A clan member born in the Sepik

K., a member of the senior living generation in his home village, had migrated to the East Sepik District, where he lived for many years, married, had three daughters and a son and died. The son, B., was raised in his mother's village, married there and had children. In 1966 (when B. was about 30) his FaSisSo, M., from his natal village in Madang visited him in the Sepik, urging him to return home to work on his land because only one youthful and lazy clan member was left. M. paid B.'s fare, and he returned to Madang without his wife and family for just over a year. Again in 1968-9 he came back for several months and half-heartedly planted coconuts as a result of M.'s exhortations. Although B. spoke only a Sepik language and Pidgin, and had considerable difficulty in adjusting to Madang and coming up to M.'s expectations, his right to land in his father's village was not questioned.

The senior active clan member is still the titular head of the clan in land matters. His position is recognized in L.T.C. hearings, and day-to-day queries are referred to him in the first instance. However, he may not make decisions without the clan *tamaniak*. Rule by consensus continues to be feasible when the average clan contains only seven adult male members. The older men are the most important in land disputes, which are fought in terms of oral history (as one informant put it: *'mipela resis long sitori'*, we compete with legends). But middle-aged and young men are often the most active in cash cropping, and in urging their fellow clansmen to undertake projects and divide land for this purpose.

A man younger than the land leader is often chosen by the clan as its L.T.C. Demarcation Committee member. Informants explained that the older man had less energy to walk long distances to meetings, was less likely to be literate and had less understanding of meeting procedure. From among the clan members are elected village, and from these, area representatives. Attendance at meetings is often regarded as onerous unless one is directly involved. But a few individuals (especially from among village and area representatives) take a great interest in all land matters, regularly attend meetings and hear, pass opinions and vote on disputes many miles from home. Such men may command considerable respect and build up valuable political capital. In the 1968 national elections a Deputy Land Titles Commissioner (also an Ambenob councillor) probably received many of the votes cast for him in the Madang/Gogol area of the Mabuso Open electorate because he was known for his land work. But such influence cannot, by the nature of its source, be electorate-wide, and he was in fact unsuccessful.

Land disputes are currently the source of great bitterness. Within clans there is friction about the allocation of land. Between them claims and counter-claims lead to strained social relationships even after an official decision has been reached. The parents of a dying child in one village sent an urgent message to a clan in another village with whom they had a land dispute to tell them to withdraw their claim and their sorcery so that the child could recover. The accused clan would accept no responsibility for the child's death, which occurred on the next day, and relations between the two groups deteriorated further. Such disputes may continue for many years. One case which came to a full hearing in the late 1960s had been the subject of ill-feeling between two villages before the Second World War.

It appears that in regular meetings of the Land Titles Commission disputes are raised more frequently between Madang villages (35 cases) than between clans of the same village (14 cases).[1] Of these 35 inter-village disputes only 9 were between villages speaking the same language, while 19 were between villages of totally different language families. Thus, given the physical distribution of languages and adjacent villages (see Appendix II, Table 24), cases within the language group are much less frequent than we would expect. Of the 11 disputes involving Madang villages which came to a full hearing before a Commissioner, all were inter-village, and all but two involved Austronesian-speaking coastal villages. This pattern of disputes raised within the formal structure of the L.T.C. may be explained by the absence of alternative mechanisms of resolution in the inter- as opposed to the intra-village context. Within the village the ethics of unity, the *tamaniak* and the numerous affinal and cognatic

---

[1] Taken from minutes of meetings of the Avisan Adjudication Area, Madang 14, between 7 June 1966 and 29 August 1968 (L.T.C., File 91-14).

ties between clans, assist informal settlement. It is precisely where
affinal and cognatic ties are most numerous (i.e. between villages
of the same language group) that inter-village disputes are referred least frequently to the L.T.C.

Controversy within the *Madang Cocoa Cooperative* mainly
concerns the proportion of profits which should be held as
reserves, reinvested, paid out in the price of wet beans or dis-
bursed as dividends and rebates.[1] The executive committee,
closely advised by the D.A.S.F., generally supports savings and
reinvestment, while shareholders are interested in ready cash,
particularly in the regular price of wet beans. The right is by no
means clearly on the side of the supervising officials. In a letter
of 30 November 1966 the Regional Agricultural Officer
criticized the District A.O. for leaving more money to be dis-
bursed at the end of the year than had been paid out to growers
during it. Lesser matters of dispute are the arrangements for the
collection of wet beans and the siting of fermentaries.

Conflict between shareholders and executive is dominated by
prominent local men who clearly have ambitions to oust office
holders in favour of themselves. Before the General Meeting in
1968 one councillor held an informal gathering of his fellow
villagers, suggested that they should want to see something for
the profits the cooperative was earning, and had the unanimous
support of his village when he unsuccessfully proposed a change
in the directors. The same councillor had previously raised
specific objections to the cooperative chairman at meetings of
the Ambenob Council Agriculture Committee. The position of
chairman is one of considerable influence on cooperative policy,
and indirectly on Administration officials. It has also in practice
been accompanied by certain perquisites.

There is no clan or village level of organization in the coopera-
tive. The decision to join is made by individual cocoa-growers.
In fact only about 60 per cent of growers are shareholders.[2]
Factors influencing the decision to join are probably the cost

---

[1] The information in this paragraph is based on D.A.S.F., File 23-3-1(2) and
my own observations at two general meetings (29 May 1968 and 6 May 1969).

[2] The number of growers is based on information in D.A.S.F. File 'Councillor
Kaut. Agricultural Committee' which contains details of the 1964 cocoa census
and in D.A.S.F. Project Areas 6 and 7, Files on individual coconut and cocoa
holdings. Membership figures are taken from Madang Cocoa Cooperative,
Register of Members.

(nearly 80 per cent of members have $30 holdings), the failure of previous cooperative ventures and the possibility of receiving the higher members' price for wet beans by deceit. In Kauris (and neighbouring Kamba) and Panim the proportion of members is high because of pressure from very pro-cooperative councillors. A feature of the cocoa cooperative (as of Pau and Bel Societies before it) is the dominance of one area. Although there are members from 50 villages, the Kamba-Kauris-Panim-Silabob block provides over one-quarter of the total membership. This group does not command a majority of votes, but it can exercise powerful pressure, especially under the leadership of the two men already mentioned.

5

The Conduct of Public Affairs

The A.L.G.C. has made a considerable departure from the traditional pattern of politically autonomous villages in that many matters concerning the village are now decided by a group of 37 councillors representing a total population of 17,000 in 131 villages. Furthermore, the position of councillor is not a village leadership role. Each councillor represents one ward (see Map 3) and an average of four villages (D.D.A., Council Elections, File 1-4). In each village there is also an elected official known in Pidgin as *komiti*. Although the English equivalent is 'ward committee member', the *komiti* in a single ward do not hold meetings together but are individually responsible to and in contact with the councillor.[2] The village is treated (e.g. for census purposes) as an indivisible unit. Although changes in ward boundaries have been made from time to time, in Madang such boundaries never divide what was traditionally a village. Between the wards and the council as a whole there is formally no intermediate grouping. But the council operates in several respects as if the wards were combined in area units. Members of the Agricultural Committee are selected on the basis of their geographical origin in such a way that they are spread evenly over the whole council area. Similarly in an election for a new member of the Executive and Finance Committee in March 1969 it was argued that one candidate was unsuitable because the councillor in the next ward was also on the same committee.

Officially foreigners resident on village land are liable for taxation to the council controlling that land at the rate of the

---

[1] In this chapter and generally in the book I am considering Ambenob Local Government Council (A.L.G.C.) before it went Multi-Racial in late 1969. However, since the elections in October 1969 were the only ones which took place during my fieldwork, I shall refer briefly to them in my account.

[2] A similar situation is recorded by Reay for the Minj-Wahgi area of the Western Highlands (1970, p. 533).

ward in which they live. In practice, however, either because of poor census records, inefficient tax collection, residential ineligibility (Papua New Guinea 1963–7, 55 (2b)) or deliberate evasion, very few labourers or members of discrete settlements of foreigners

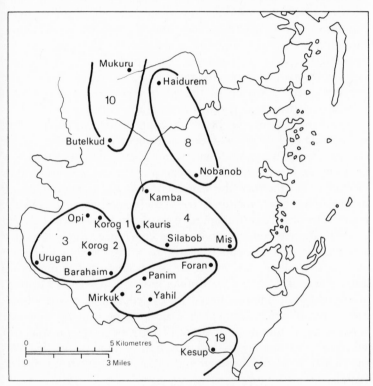

Map 3. Wards of the 1967/69 Ambenob Local Government Council for the 17 villages only

pay up. For example, only 3 out of 40 adult men in one settlement pay taxes to Ambenob. 'Friends and affines' resident with kinsmen are much more likely to do so, especially when their home is also within the Ambenob area. Labourers and residents of foreign settlements play little part in council affairs at the village level. Often they do not help with village tasks such as road maintenance. One informant grumbled, 'I'm thinking of moving them on. Some of them are disobedient. They won't

work with the village. They won't pay taxes.' Foreigners of this
type are also disinclined to attend village meetings. In fact
councillors often have to visit and address such settlements separately if they want to make contact with them at all. Villagers
and foreigners alike feel that the village meeting is the landowners' *tamaniak*, and that they alone have the right to make
decisions there. Councillors sometimes try to alter this situation,
though whether to muster more support for themselves or for
democratic reasons is debatable. Thus one councillor regularly
ordered his own labourers to attend village meetings, and on one
occasion made a speech to the effect that they were as much
involved in Ambenob Council as were the villagers.

Another element in the relationship between council and
settlements of foreigners is the resentment and hostility which
often exists between landowners and guests. At times unhappy
landowners even attempt to persuade the council to use its
powers to rid them of the settlements. At the General Meeting
in December 1968 members from the coastal area wanted the
council to drive out foreigners who did not pay taxes. As far
as occupation of official positions is concerned, foreigners play
a negligible part in council affairs. In a bye-election in March
1969, a councillor was elected for his home ward while living
away from it (A.L.G.C., Minute No. 7-2, General Meeting,
10 April 1969), but was urged by the council to return home.
However, all other councillors appear to be land-owning and
resident ward members. I know of only one case (in Silabob)
where a previous *komiti* had not been a landowner. He was
married to a Silabob woman and came originally from Karkar
Island.

Although the ward is the unit of direct representation in the
council chamber, it appears that it has not in fact become established as much more than this. The ward as a whole does not
usually participate in joint activities. Councillors visit each of
their villages in turn, and hold separate meetings in each to report
council decisions and ascertain the wishes of the people. The
most obvious reason for holding single village meetings is that
only one man need walk to a meeting place. Councillors realize
that people are more likely to attend a meeting near at hand
than one at a distance. Their opinion is borne out by the council
election turnout in Wards 2, 3 and 4 in 1969, where proportion-

ately between two and three times as many people voted from the three villages where the polling booths were located than from the others (figures taken from A.L.G.C., Ward Voting Registers). Tax Payers' Meetings are only held once a year, and usually combine more than one ward in a central meeting. In January 1969, for example, only 14 meetings were held for the 37 wards. Wards rarely work as units on particular projects. A village is responsible for its own hygiene, and the maintenance of tracks and roads on its land. Although adjacent villages do sometimes cooperate, they may not necessarily come from the same ward. Korog and Kauris men laid pipes together on the road between their two villages in May 1968.

The village is also a much more genuine interest group than the ward. Since the council is largely a means of attracting central Administration funds to the area, and of encouraging people to pool resources for projects which small groups would separately be unable to finance, local contributions and council expenditure are inevitably the burning political issues.[1] There is keen public interest in personal tax levels, tax exemptions, tax differentials between wards, and contributions in kind (mainly labour) to self-help projects. These matters are perceived largely as concerning the village rather than the ward. For example, one informant in Ward 3 claimed that, although other villages in his ward might be able to afford $9.00 tax because they were nearer the road, his own people in Opi could not pay so much. Similarly council expenditure is seen as largely benefiting particular villages rather than wards – given that villages are comparatively territorially compact. The money available for such expenditure is in any case limited by revenue, personal emoluments and recurring costs, the latter two accounting for 73 per cent of expenditure in the 1969/70 Draft Estimates (A.L.G.C., Minutes of Executive and Finance Special Meeting, 3 March 1969). What little money there is can only benefit a tiny minority of villages in any one year. Thus the estimates already quoted provided for expenditure on roads serving at most 10, and on water supplies for 4, of the 131 villages. It is therefore the village and not the ward which attempts to act as a pressure group to direct council funds into a particular area. Thus Kamba village

---

[1] Necessarily such issues are prominent in local government systems in many parts of the world. For an African example see Leys 1967, esp. Chapters 4, 5 and 6.

in 1968 had a special bank account containing $300 designed partly to shame the council into producing their long-awaited feeder road. Feeling in Kamba ran very high on this matter, as can be seen from the following tirade by one of their representatives at a Tax Payers' Meeting in January 1969:

> I, I am a Kamba. I am a man from the bush.
> I sleep in a hole on rocks. We don't have
> a road. I'm like a woman. I wear a grass skirt.
> I hear the fame of the coastal people. But you
> have struck me down. I have nothing to say.

It should perhaps be added that in the council chamber itself most issues are not hotly debated. In 14 General Meetings between July 1968 and August 1969, 126 out of 132 non-procedural motions were carried unanimously (from duplicated Pidgin minutes) and none of the six contested motions concerned tax rates or capital expenditure. The general lack of dissension can be attributed to heavy reliance on an executive committee, informal discussion outside the council chamber, the traditional ethic of consensus, councillors' failure to understand what is happening and the use of the council as an instrument of administration by the central government. For this last reason Administration officials, especially in the earlier part of my fieldwork, 'guided' events fairly forcefully.[1]

The overshadowing of the ward politically has also contributed to the failure of the councillor as a ward rather than a village leadership role. A similar trend against multi-village leadership has been recorded for an earlier period by Rowley (1954, p. 775) in connection with the failure of the German Union system. The councillor is perceived and operates largely as a village official. In a village which has no councillor, the *komiti* acts as an unpaid deputy, performs the duties and has almost the status of councillor. It is the *komiti* who supervises the Monday labour on roads, aid posts and school grounds. It is the *komiti* who receives visiting Administration officials and who guides such men through census revision and the hearing of disputes. Sometimes the councillor may also be present, but he is less important than the *komiti*. *Komiti* may attend General Meetings of the council as

---

[1] For a similar situation in the Northern District see Crocombe 1968, pp. 131–4.

observers. They are supposed to attend in the absence of the councillor, and the council often relies on *komiti* to report the feelings or complaints of their fellow villagers. On one occasion the council asked a councillor who reported trouble in his ward to bring along the *komiti* from the village concerned to explain the problem (A.L.G.C., Minute No. 11-1, General Meeting, 5 August 1968). At Tax Payers' Meetings too *komiti* often report the wishes of their villages, and are sometimes called upon by the President to do so. In minor disputes it is the *komiti* rather than the councillor who is the first point of reference in villages other than the councillor's own. However the *komiti* may refer the case later to the councillor, or at least notify him. In the councillor's own village, the *komiti* has less responsibility, rarely speaking on behalf of the village, occasionally deputizing for the councillor, and sometimes being the first point of reference in a dispute, as in Case 3 below.

Case 3. The widow's sugar cane

On the morning of Friday 7 June 1968 the village *komiti*, his brother and B. visited the councillor in their village. They reported that that morning an old widow of the village, S., had gone to her garden to collect food to send to her absent son-in-law. Certain food which she had had in mind to send was missing. She accused B. of stealing her sugar cane, and also of taking other food from the garden of J., her HusclanBroSo. (B. is a notorious food thief, being a lazy gardener and having six children.) She also accused B. of assisting J.'s wife to run away and leave him. Then J.'s father, T. (who was also held responsible for alienating J.'s wife), and J.'s clan brother, K., came up and remonstrated with B. about being rude to S. and grabbing her by the hand. A fight broke out and B. got cut around the face.

On hearing this news the councillor appeared very angry, and sent them all to the police in town, saying 'It's no good my telling people things, they never take any notice'. About 3 p.m. four police came to the village and took the three combatants to town. At the police station the whole affair was discussed, the three shook hands and were allowed to return home.

There is also a widespread feeling that village interests are best served by a councillor from one's own village (or, at second best, by one from another village with strong affinal links). To this end, many villages hold meetings or informally discuss forthcoming elections and thereby attempt to reduce the number

G

of nominations so that the village vote is not split. Thus in the 1967 and 1969 elections, a large proportion of multi-village wards (30 out of 42) did not put forward more than one candidate from the same village.[1]

An index of the relative significance of ward and village unity is the disputes which have arisen in Ambenob (although outside the villages under study) over ward boundaries. At a General Meeting in June 1969 a councillor reported that some of his people were not in agreement with the proposed revision of ward boundaries, because they would be in the same ward as a village with which they had long-standing land disputes. When the Advising Officer suggested that the council was not concerned with land, the councillor replied that damage to crops and removal of demarcation pegs were also involved. The speech of another councillor can be summarized here: 'Ward boundaries are for administrative purposes. It's not a question of villages doing things together. It's just a matter of what the councillor will be doing. If we obey people's whims they will carry on like this over and over again.' The objections were overruled.

Apart from the occasional formal recognition of area interests mentioned earlier in this chapter, the geographical origin of councillors has certain other implications for the operation of the council. It appears that councillors from the Amele (between the Gum and Gogol), Nobanob (Big Name Wagi) and Bel (Austronesian-speaking) areas dominate the proceedings at the expense of those from further inland. The first (appointed) President was the old paramount *luluai* of Amele village itself. He was followed by a Lutheran pastor from nearby Hilu. The Vice-Presidents have come from Riwo (Bel), Panim (Nobanob), Kranket (Bel), Riwo (Bel) and Bilbil (Bel). Similarly the Executive and Finance Committee has regularly favoured the same areas, apparently on the ground that travelling was too difficult for more distant councillors.

The dominance of Ambenob by certain areas is partly a result of history, in that such areas have provided the founding, and therefore today the most experienced members of the council. In terms of their years of service the councillors fall into two main groups – 10 who have been with Ambenob since its inception

[1] A.L.G.C., Election files, Form D: Voting Statistics (1967) and Direction 36, Form 11: Voting Summary (1969).

and 14 who were first elected in 1967 (11 of these were from trans-Gogol and far inland wards which were only added in that year). The dominant areas are also those with the highest general level of education and contact with town and expatriates, whose councillors have more confidence and expertise in council affairs. In addition, councillors from these areas know each other better through council work, common church interests and affinal links than they know the newcomers from more distant areas. One member of the Executive and Finance Committee in 1968 could not name a single councillor from south of the Gogol. Thus the councillors from the remote areas have minimal formal or informal influence on council decisions.

Ambenob Council does not appear to have created a feeling of unity among the people in its area. This is partly a result of the generally poor public image of the council (see below) and partly a result of the fact that the council is not perceived as a pressure group in a more inclusive political arena. Although each council is competing for funds with others in its district, and ultimately in Papua New Guinea as a whole, councillors see themselves – quite rightly – as having negligible control over the allocation of such funds. The District Conference, at which each council is represented, appears to discuss mainly matters of common interest to all councils. Ambenob contributed only one agenda item in 1969, and that was on the question of pensions for long-serving councillors (D.D.A., District Councils Conference, Madang District). Nor does the District Advisory Council attract much attention from councillors or the public, although it certainly occasionally discusses agenda items submitted by the President. All requests to the D.A.C. for capital assistance between 1962 and 1967 were unsuccessful. Thus at a meeting on 25 May 1966 Ambenob was told to buy itself a new ferry if it wanted one (D.D.A., District Advisory Council. File 1-14-4).

The council has failed to provide a viable sense of common purpose and mutual responsibility. A man believes that his tax money should directly benefit himself, and if possible other people's taxes should also help him. There is little idea of a welfare state or of richer helping poorer, ideas rare enough in many developed countries, but in the case of Ambenob not even the surface ethics, or as Bailey (1969, p. 5) has called them 'the normative rules', have become universalized. There are one or two exceptions to this generalization, among them a councillor who spoke substantially as follows:

At Tax Payers' Meetings we must write down what people ask for. Projects must be listed on the blackboard at Danben [council H.Q.]. We must be fair with our expenditures. We must spread the money around. One year in one village, one year in another. Not always in one village.

The role of councillor was selected for special study in preference to that of *komiti* both because once a month all councillors were to be found in one place at one time and because, operating as they do in an inter-village arena, they are perhaps more closely linked to the modern political structure. Informants named two overriding characteristics as being desirable in a councillor. One (and in this they said they followed the views of the local government officer who introduced the council in 1956) is that the councillor should be like an old *luluai* or *tultul*, steady and respected, able to keep order and to make wise decisions on disputes in the village. The second characteristic frequently mentioned is that the councillor should be able to 'talk out at Danben', to carry the words of the people to the council chamber. While the first characteristic refers to qualities exercised largely within the village and ward, and has certain parallels in traditional leadership roles, the second calls for skills in dealing with people beyond the village – oratory, good Pidgin, possibly some education and experience in dealing with expatriates and the Administration – and is oriented towards a new rather than an older order.

Sometimes a ward is fortunate enough to have men who satisfy both of these popular requirements but often it must choose between them. Some wards deliberately place higher value on one or other of the requirements. It is often said of the coastal wards that they elect younger, educated men who are articulate in council meetings but are subservient to the elders of their villages who remain responsible for social control at home. Further inland, partially, one must admit of necessity, the people elect councillors who follow much more closely the traditional leadership pattern of the respected and wise village elder, and select men who are inept in the council chamber. In part this contributes to the imbalance of power between areas described above.

I briefly interviewed each of the 37 councillors in office in 1968. It was difficult to ascertain ages without a knowledge of each local area, but I estimate that the average age of councillors is somewhere between 40 and 50 years, only one councillor being under 30. All 37 speak Pidgin, but only 4 are able to understand some English. Nine are unable to read or write. Table 9 shows that

Table 9. Experience of councillors before their first election to office

Position	No. of councillors
(a) *Administration and other secular organizations*	
medical assistant	6
tultul	5
komiti	4
luluai	4
chairman/director or Rural Progress Society or Cooperative	3
clerk of same	2
D.A.S.F. employee	2
police	2
council carpenter	1
council clerk	1
council road foreman	1
Japanese local official	1
President P. and C.	1
Vice-President M.W.A.	1
(b) *Mission*	
teacher	7
elder/headman	4
pastor	2
plantation foreman	1
(c) *None of above*	7

the majority of councillors have held positions of responsibility with the Administration or a mission. In this table 14 councillors have occupied more than one position each. In Chapter 7 I discuss the current relationship between other leadership roles and that of councillor. As shown in Table 10, a considerable number of councillors have invested in commercial projects. In addition to those councillors shown in the table, three more had income from casual employment. A total of 13 councillors had no source of income or commercial investment apart from the produce they sold at the market in Madang Town. These few figures suggest that, in terms of literacy, leadership experience and commercial interests (especially in relation to coconuts, a relatively heavy-investment crop), many of the councillors may be rather unusual men in their wards. This is borne out by informants and of course by the fact of their election. But although a number of councillors may have certain characteristics in common, when they are in the council chamber there are wide variations between them in performance. Many councillors play little or no part in what happens in the council chamber, while action is dominated by five or six men. In General Meetings in 1968,[1] 92 out of 119 motions were proposed by a total of five

Table 10. Commercial interests of councillors

Investment in	No. of councillors
cocoa	11
coconuts	15
coffee	2
rice	1
hens	1
clay pots	1
trade store	1

councillors, while 63 out of 109 new matters were raised by only four (including three of the earlier group). At the other end of the spectrum, seven members are not recorded as having taken any active part in meetings, although admittedly lengthy discussions are not recorded in the minutes. Another five members have never proposed a motion or raised new business. These very wide contrasts arise from temperamental differences (associated with the two models of what a councillor should be like), variations in experience both on and off the council, uneven educational background and the degree to which any individual has personal contacts with other councillors which assure him of support or at least a fair hearing. For such reasons it is the councillors from

[1] Information taken from A.L.G.C., Minutes of General Meetings for 1968. These excluded the June meeting, for which no minutes were available, and included one Special Meeting on 21 August.

the trans-Gogol and far inland wards who generally participate least in council affairs. Nine of the 12 who say little or nothing in the council chamber come from the two areas just mentioned.

Another result of this pattern of selection is that, even by Madang standards, the councillors are a politically conservative group.[1] Councillors argue that Papua New Guinea is not yet ready for independence because it needs Australian experience, skills, investment and aid. As one put it in the General Meeting in February 1969, 'The government must not leave the council too quickly.' Some councillors regard the withdrawal of Australian support as synonymous with acute poverty and anarchy. These attitudes can be explained in a number of ways. Councillors are on the whole older men who have grown up in a more rigidly colonial situation than that of today. Many have seen service in positions of undemocratic subordination to colonial masters (e.g. as *luluai*). The council is closely guided by the Administration, and members are used to being the mouthpieces for official policy and information, much of the latter unrelated to local affairs. Thus messages about adult education, women's clubs, the South Pacific Games and the Madang Annual Festival of Music were relayed from the Administration through the councillors at General Meetings in January, March, May and July 1969 respectively. It is hardly surprising therefore that there is not much of a tradition of deviation from official policy, especially on such an important issue as independence (for a statement of the official anti-independence line see speech by the Minister for External Territories reported in *The Australian*, 20 December 1968). It might also be argued that councillors see a preservation of the *status quo* as in their own personal interests, while younger, better-educated and more forward-looking men who might think differently are not so likely to get elected, especially in those areas voting in terms of traditional leadership roles. The cream of the younger men, and those least likely to be politically conservative are absent from the villages altogether. Villagers are not in touch with them, or with the comparatively radical elites in the towns because of their own illiteracy, and the difficulties of communication between the large centres and the villages.

Councillors enjoy several perquisites. They all receive *honoraria*

[1] For a more general discussion of these issues see Postscript 1972.

of $4 per month, and there are additional payments for member-
ship of committees and patrols. Through their job councillors
have considerable informal contact with Administration officials,
from whom they often receive valuable advice (e.g. about
personal financial affairs) as well as prestigious invitations (e.g. to
tea at the District Commissioner's). The council employs labour,
and councillors can channel these opportunities in any direction
they choose. Many of the employees at council headquarters were
personally known to councillors before their appointment.
Thus a temporary typist appointed at the April General Meeting
in 1969 was a personal friend of one councillor, who was also a
Lutheran church worker, and had recently left his job at the
headquarters of the Amele Circuit. Temporary road labour
(at $6 per fortnight) is directly recruited by each councillor for
projects in his own ward. One councillor, whose own recruitment seemed fair, said, 'It's up to individuals. If they want to
work they can.' But there nevertheless seems some room for
partiality here. Councillors also have hotly disputed[1] access to
council vehicles, transport being a very scarce commodity in the
Ambenob area. Within his own village, the councillor has
considerable *de facto* control over the distribution of tax exemptions since these are granted by a Review Committee in meetings
with the applicants at which the councillor is often the only
other person with local knowledge. The councillor can also
omit to draw to the attention of the compilers of the tax register
the names of labourers and other foreigners who are theoretically
liable. In their own villages and beyond, the councillors are
addressed by their title and many enjoy considerable local
prestige. On one occasion I saw a councillor's brother, son and
older men of his village carry baggage, while he himself strolled
along empty-handed in knee-socks and highly polished shoes.
Through patrols and committee work a councillor may become
well-known over a wide area and, according to his competence,
respected. The way in which being a councillor can be a stepping-
stone to another career is discussed in Chapter 7.

But the councillor's job also has its drawbacks. Patrols and
meetings occupy a considerable amount of his time and energies.
Two councillors told me they hoped to retire at the 1969 elections

[1] Apparently council transport is also a matter of concern to councillors
elsewhere in New Guinea (see Reay 1970, pp. 542–3 and Strathern 1970, p. 560).

1. Yali in December 1970. I prefer this to some of my earlier pictures because it shows some of the old leader's charm and humour.

2. Yali at Sor in late 1970 with a group of *lo bos* who had come to help him celebrate the new year. Most of the *lo bos* are not from the Rai Coast and the group includes the itinerant secretary from Kauris.

3. Yakob, a photograph taken in 1969 at Mawan village where he was performing rituals similar to those performed in Madang.

4. Children performing Yakob's money-making ritual. Yakob (seated) watches them as each dips his finger into a cup containing water, 10¢ and Yakob's semen collected the previous night. Each child flicks the liquid around his face in the form of a cross. Later the children go to pre-arranged sites in the forest to find coins. (Note the jar of leaves copied from Yali's ritual.)

5. The house built of permanent materials owned by one of the wealthiest Madangs.

6. Weighing wet beans on the Madang Cocoa Cooperative truck. Cash is paid on the spot, cooperative members receiving a higher price than non-members.

7. The Lutheran church in Nobanob village.

8. A General Meeting of Ambenob Local Government Council. At this meeting the President was absent and the chair was taken by the Vice-President. Budget estimates can be seen on the blackboard.

9. Mr Angmai Bilas, M.H.A. for Mabuso Open, addressing a meeting at Mis in October 1968. At this meeting the M.H.A. spoke of his work and the functions of the House of Assembly, and heard villagers' views and complaints. The councillor for Ward 4 (seated) was in the chair.

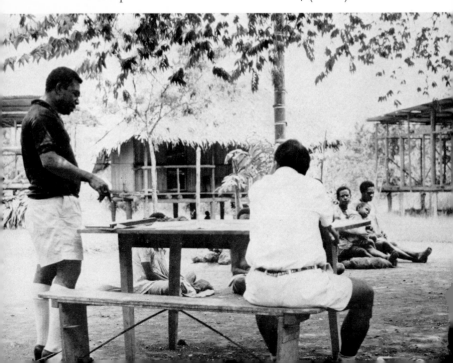

to devote more time to commercial development of their land. Another ex-councillor told me he had given up because he did not have a close kinsman to help him out with the work he was unable to do at home. Councillors are often caught between the people on the one hand and the Administration and the council on the other. For example, councillors were sent to one village by the District Commissioner to enquire who would be prepared to sell land to the Administration, a highly unpopular request. Again, Portfolio Members of the council are held personally responsible for shortcomings in their programmes which are often not their fault at all.

Unpopular instructions move downwards to the village and impossible demands move upwards. The councillor is in the middle. An ex-councillor complained to me about the admonitory role of councillor: 'I didn't tell people off. I wasn't angry with people. I followed the custom of my ancestors.' But at the same time councillors feel the necessity to impress the council and Administration officials with the energy, loyalty and smooth running of their wards. One councillor organized a far from rousing performance of the national anthem to greet the District Commissioner at a Tax Payers' Meeting. One of the councillors' biggest worries is the absence of legal sanctions against villagers who do not maintain roads or keep medical aid posts clean. The matter is raised frequently in the council chamber. Thus at the General Meeting in March 1969 the Portfolio Member for Public Works grumbled about villagers who did not clear the drains and edges of their roads. In the ensuing discussion one councillor lamented the passing of the *luluai/tultul* system in which officials had authority to coerce villagers.

Although the councillor has no judicial authority, he does try to handle minor disputes. Serious offences must be referred directly to the police. Sometimes two councillors try to sort out a case involving parties from both their wards. In some instances a councillor will discuss a dispute with only the parties involved, while in others he may be one of many contributors to the discussions of the *tamaniak* of his own clan or village. The councillor has however no sanctions except reference to an external authority. Case 3, the widow's sugar-cane, provided an example of almost instant reference, while in Case 4 (below) a councillor's intervention was more successful. In general the differences between the two cases can be traced to the different personal relations between councillor and parties.

Case 4. A disgruntled wife

On Saturday 19 October 1968, S. of K. village told me that he had heard at the market a rumour that his wife, A., had been having an affair with B. of neighbouring S. village. The following Tuesday S. beat his wife soundly for this suspected adultery. On the Wednesday the two *komiti* from S. and K. villages and the councillor (of K. village) held a meeting of the parties concerned in K. village. B.'s wife (G.) was there and she sounded off with a whole string of complaints against her husband, including his adultery on two occasions. Other complaints were that he had used the money she had saved for buying kerosene to pay people who had helped him cut down forest and as a gift to a single girl; that he had beaten her; that he didn't help take her sick child to the aid post and when she eventually went into hospital with the child B. visited and brought her food only at irregular intervals. When asked if she had herself witnessed her husband's adultery, G. said that two other men had told her about it.

The husband replied that he was furious when she had accused him of giving her kerosene money to the unmarried girl and explained again how he had spent the money. On the accusations of adultery, he said that there had been many people with him and A. at her husband's house on one of the nights in question, and as for the other occasion he had no alibi but would abide by the decision of the meeting. An intermediary was then sent to ask A. what she had to say. She replied that she had never committed adultery with B.

Then the councillor summed up:

There is just gossip here, no adultery. But, B., you and G. are not getting along very well. You must improve. That's why other people got talking. The problem is just B. and G.'s. Other people shouldn't join in with gossip . . . The best thing is for B. and S. to shake hands with each other and exchange five shillings. A. and G. can do the same.

This was done and the meeting concluded.

Foreigners who are related directly to village members by marriage etc. do not appear to pose law and order problems significantly different from those of villagers themselves (but see Case 5 below for an exception). As one councillor said, 'We can handle men related by marriage to a local village. The others are difficult.' Where there are no affinal ties to further mutual understanding and mediation, where the *tamaniak* has no jurisdiction, where the councillor, pastor and *lo bos* are ill at ease, in other words in the discrete settlements of foreigners, to village eyes there is a deplorable breakdown in social order. Thus one councillor complained at the December General Meeting in 1968 about theft and illicit dealings with village women from a settlement on his land. Hired labourers on the other hand are usually very much under the thumb of their employer, while the plantations are not such a problem either because of their geographical discreteness. But there are troubles with people living on pockets of alienated land within village boundaries, for instance in schools. One school was closed for several months after a severe disagreement between headmaster and village over the love affairs of his domestic servant. Further sources of trouble are improved road communications and the proximity of Madang Town. A number of road workers, truck and grader drivers and party-goers from town often visit the villages for a few hours and cause havoc among the more susceptible women. Villagers have almost no control over such people except through the police and courts.

Strathern (1970, p. 561) has suggested that in a council in the Western Highlands, 'Where councillors *could* get their people to work, it was clear that their indigenously-based power was propping up or "subsidising" the council system.' Although in Madang, with a much longer period of contact, 'indigenously-based power' is absent in its pure form, in order to be successful both in and after elections Madang councillors do 'subsidize' their role as formally defined. I have already mentioned the potential influence of a councillor on employment, tax exemptions and the registration of foreigners for taxation purposes. A councillor can also fail to report other irregularities to the council or call in the police on disputes, options well known to be open to him. These favours can be judiciously distributed. For instance, one councillor was particularly careful not to antagonize further people who were already hostile to him. He did not challenge one of these when he applied for tax exemption on the grounds of poor eyesight, though in fact the man's eyes were only weak at night and so had no effect on his earning capacity. A councillor can also use his financial resources in both traditional forms of assistance and in new ways. One councillor paid out $90 for tax defaulters in his village in 1969. He explicitly said this was so they could all be at peace with one another and they would not resent prosecution and imprisonment. It also meant that nine potentially rebellious men were in his debt. The personal qualities of a councillor – oratory, persuasiveness, intelligence etc. – will assist him in his task. If he attracts council funds to his area he will be more popular than if he does not. Further, as with Strathern's Big Men-councillors in the Highlands, a man who has standing and influence in the community – either in modern or traditional roles – in some ways distinct from his position as councillor will be able to fill that role more effectively (see Chapter 7).

Ties of kinship and affinity can also serve to subsidize the councillor's role. He can usually count on support from his clansmen and other cognates and affines, either because their prestige is involved with his, because of other indebtedness, because he is likely to support them against others or because they hope for future favours. Such ties are particularly important for the councillor in his relationship with other villages than his own. For example, one councillor for a two-village ward is regularly elected unopposed. One of the reasons given by informants is that his wife comes from the other village and he has close and amiable relations with his in-laws. Similarly in one election in October 1969, when an informant was evaluating candidates' chances, he assumed that a man's wife's village from which there was no alternative candidate would vote for him. The importance of such inter-village ties can also be seen in attendance at meetings, hospitality within the ward and the reference of disputes to the councillor. In Case 5 a councillor was consulted about a dispute from another village because of kinship ties.

Case 5. A divorce from a foreigner

T., a man from the Sepik District, had married K. a Madang woman in 1966 and settled in her village. He paid no brideprice and did little work for his father-in-law, S. There were many quarrels between T. and K. Once T. left her and then returned. K. accused him of attacking her with a knife and axe.

On 9 May 1968 S. and T.'s village patron/host came to see the councillor for their ward (from another village). The councillor was S.'s FaMoSisSoSo and it was at least partly on these grounds, the councillor told me, that the case had been referred to him. S. said he had been to the police who had sent him to his councillor. It was decided that K. should come and stay with the councillor's brother so that the councillor could keep an eye on her.

On 13 May there was another meeting at the councillor's house attended by the councillor, K., T., T.'s friend and a senior clansman of the councillor. T. said he did not like the wife his friend, a Sepik already married into the same village, had found him. In turn the friend accused him of laziness. The councillor summed up the case as follows:

You are both to blame . . . The law of Wagi is that a man buys his wife . . . Anyway, it is up to you both to decide what you want. The best thing would be if you both left the village and K.'s husband found work in Madang or on a plantation, or even paid the bride-price and went home to the Sepik. If you find a job you can come back later and help your wife's father and mother. If you can't find a house, K. will have to stay in the village. If you behave badly I'll send you to court and they'll send you back to the Sepik. You must work hard in the village and plant coconuts on your wife's land.

T. said he could not find work in Madang and did not want to go back to the Sepik. So the councillor concluded:

I'd like to see for myself how you behave, so right now you go and get your things. Tomorrow come and sleep with my brother here.

The next day both started living together as arranged in the councillor's hamlet. But it was not many weeks later that the husband left the village for town and, after one or two odd visits, left K. permanently.

Ambenob Council has to contend with considerable apathy among its voters and tax payers. This can be seen in the 38 per cent turnout at the 1969 elections (D.D.A. (Special) Patrol Report 6 of 1969/70, Madang District) and a total attendance of only about 1,500 at Tax Payers' Meetings (D.D.A., File 42-4-2). But there are certain indications that the public attitude might be described as dissatisfaction rather than apathy. There is a rising number of tax defaulters, and Tax Payers' Meetings are full of open criticisms of the council; for example at Amron (Haidurem): 'Ambenob Council is just a name. The people are angry.' Some even advocate a return to the *luluai* and *tultul* system (D.D.A., File 42-4-2). Council officials are uneasily aware of such attitudes. The Adviser wrote in his Annual Report in 1968 (D.D.A., File 42-4-2) 'Generally, the people of the council area do not seem pleased with the council', and in the February General Meeting in 1969 a councillor said: 'The people are really not happy with the council's work . . .They are very worried. They have no faith in the council's work.' In Kamba village matters came to a head in January 1969, when many men chose to go before the stipendiary magistrate in Madang Town to be tried for tax default. Public opinion was '*Ol i laik traim kaunsil nau. Ol i laik kotim kaunsil.* (Now they are testing the council. They are taking the council to court.)' Although these statements do not describe the legal situation, they do reflect the Kambas' reasons for having their cases heard in town rather than by a D.D.A. official in the village, and convey the spirit in which they attended their hearings. To a man the Kamba protesters eventually found themselves in Be'on Corrective Institution after again refusing to pay up. This situation has certain parallels with the position of the local government council in the Minj-Wahgi area of the Western Highlands District. Reay (1970, p. 544) suggests that there was a lack of 'legitimacy' in Weber's sense, a description which appears particularly appropriate in Madang too in view of the Kamba tax courts.

The causes of the council's unpopularity are various. In 1956 and 1957 many people in the area had unrealistic (cargo-type) hopes of what the new council might achieve. One informant clearly explained present dissatisfaction in such terms when he said, 'When we wanted to start the council Mr P. [D.D.A. officer responsible] said "you will get good houses and live like us [expatriates]". So now we young people are rebellious because our fathers didn't get what was promised.' As the council has grown in size, communication with the people has become rarer and more perfunctory, and the council is seen as unresponsive to public opinion especially on questions of tax rates and expenditure. In fact financial management has been unsatisfactory in a number of respects. In the years 1967/68 and 1968/69, only $3,990 was spent at village level while $13,190 went on items (excluding a road grader worth $13,000) retained at council headquarters (D.D.A., File 42-4-2). In 1968/69 a large number of works projects including three roads, a bridge, two clinics and a pump were proposed in early estimates and later deleted because of over-estimation of expenditure and tax default. This caused much bitterness in the wards. Because of their relatively low levels of education and the complexities of the budgets and bureaucracy they are handling, the councillors often rely heavily on the Adviser and permanent council staff. This has led to public suspicion that the councillors are not running their own show ('the council is no good because it is under the thumb of the government') and a greater feeling of popular alienation from the control of events. At the same time heavy responsibilities are placed on the Advising Officer's shoulders. His performance is often hampered by the rapidity of transfers in the public service, and sometimes by incompetence. For example, in the General Meeting of March 1969, a D.D.A. official publicly blamed a previous Advising Officer for wasting $5,000 of council money on a saw which proved to be of no use to the council.

PARENTS AND CITIZENS' ASSOCIATIONS

As mentioned in Chapter 2, Parents and Citizens' Associations support the schools in the area with labour, funds and fund-raising activities. Since the A.L.G.C. General Meeting of October 1968, they have also appointed an inter-village truancy officer for each school to chase up children who are regularly absent. The appointment of these officers is ratified by the council. The officer does not necessarily come from the village in which the school is situated. For example, in 1968 a Korog man was appointed for Barahaim School. There is also an elected committee, which usually contains representatives from most villages in the school's area. Although all parents and interested villagers are eligible to join the P. and C.'s, the active membership often comes mainly from the village in which the school is built. This leads to a considerable amount of resentment in the home village over the contribution made by other villages. All are expected to send men to help in the maintenance of school grounds and at parties etc., but many do not send help as often or as generously as the home village would like. In desperation in 1968, Barahaim P. and C. made a rule that parents who failed to show up for the Thursday working bees would have to pay 60¢ for every day they missed.

POLICE AND COURTS

In the eyes of many villagers, the police operate independently of the courts and magistrates, and can themselves pass judgements

and enforce decisions. This idea is due partly to ignorance
partly to *ultra vires* actions by individual policemen, and partly
to police mediation in minor disputes (as in Case 3). The police
are seen as particularly capable of handling physically awkward
situations such as drunken brawls, and so they are invited to
and do in fact attend many of the large fund-raising parties held
in the area on Saturday nights. They are also called out in cases
where one party deliberately absents himself from hearings or
will not voluntarily come to any form of mediation. Villagers
perceive the police largely as a number of individuals with some
of whom they have personal relationships of friendship or enmity.
Some are seen as approachable and even manipulable, and
villagers deliberately choose the person with whom they will
lay their complaint.

There is a certain amount of friction over jurisdiction between
council and police. In 1968 the Advising Officer wrote: 'Relations
with police have been strained due to the apparent overlap of
functions within the Madang Police zone which includes Ambenob. Regular police patrols move within the area, but continually meddle in affairs of purely council responsibility' (D.D.A.,
File 42-4-2). At the council meeting in September 1968, there
were complaints of a row between the Health Committee and
the police over the former's right to order people to rebuild
dilapidated houses.

In theory all kinds of minor as well as major offences are
covered by the courts, but in practice a very small number of
these ever get there. Even councillors, who are supposed to
bring serious matters to the attention of the courts, often do not
know what cases *must* be referred to them. I questioned several
councillors about an accident with a school bus in which several
children had been killed. Most of them thought it was all right
for a witness or a parent to kill the driver on the spot, and that
such a killing would not have been punishable by a court. In
fact the driver knew very well what the local reaction would be,
and had immediately made himself so scarce that many months
after the accident he had not been brought to book. The decision
to go to court is usually taken either by an individual, a councillor
or a *tamaniak*, only when a favourable judgement is expected.
Thus in cases of dispute over marriage arrangements the young
people are usually more anxious to go to court than their parents,

because they know the court is likely to uphold their freedom of choice.

A number of people and institutions are involved in the maintenance of social order – the *tamaniak*, the police, the courts, the councillor, the *lo bos*, the pastor and through various kinds of self-help the common man. There is very little, if any, concept of *obligation* to refer a dispute or misdemeanour to any particular authority. There is hardly a sense in which a man, especially if he is of low status and has little influence, is obliged to do anything at all if he has been wronged. In fact *not* doing anything can be an element in the mental ledger of debts and credits in a particular relationship between two men, and can give one a future advantage over the other. However people have the *option* to act in a number or a combination of different ways. Their decision will depend on their calculation of their own advantage, the publicity given to the matter (e.g. reporting to the councillor) and decisions taken by the other party. They may try self-help in the first instance, especially where there is not a long history of ill-will, and if that fails they may go to a councillor or to court. The police may refer a case back to a councillor or to the welfare officer. The *tamaniak* can decide to send an unresolved case to court, or ask a magistrate to ratify a decision it has reached. Thus a divorce, re-marriage and compensation were agreed by the *tamaniak* of one village and ratified by an administrative officer (Silabob Village Book, 9 October 1962). The *tamaniak* may also estimate the chances that a court will give the decision they want. For example, at one meeting to discuss a man's adultery with his son's wife, the *tamaniak* agreed that it would have been a good case for a magistrate had not the issue been complicated by the woman's desertion of her husband.

The clan and village *tamaniak* have become less important for social control in the face of external institutions to which people can appeal. The courts and police operate according to principles not always shared by villagers, and make decisions often uninfluenced by public opinion. In traditional times, if a man wanted effectively to help himself or obtain public redress, he had to have the support of his own group (*tamaniak*) and/or other kinsmen. Today he can go to court against the advice of everyone else and possibly get his own way. In the present system of social control in Madang, therefore, individual

H

independence is considerably greater than it was in the traditional system.

THE HOUSE OF ASSEMBLY[1]

Because the national House of Assembly plays a comparatively minor role in day-to-day local politics, and because I did not myself witness the 1968 elections, I did not make a special study of it. Here, as throughout the book, my comments are restricted largely to the 17 villages under study. However, Peter Lawrence and his team studied the 1968 national elections in the whole Mabuso, Rai Coast and Sumkar Open electorates and the corresponding parts of the Madang Regional (Harding and Lawrence 1971). I am indebted to their work in some of what follows.

Although the House of Assembly was established in 1964, the villagers' knowledge of it continues to be very limited. The phrase 'Haus Asembli' is widely known, but very few people are able to say that it is a council for the whole of Papua New Guinea. In some quarters one fears misconceptions as well as ignorance, particularly among followers of Yali. His supporters described the House to me in various terms. According to them its main feature is the door which only Yali can open. One lo bos told me the door has whirling swords on it which will only rest when Yali approaches. When this door is opened wealth will pour out to all New Guinea. As one supporter told me, 'We elected Suguman [M.H.A. 1964–8] and he went to the House of Assembly. He didn't go inside. I think he didn't know the secret of the House.' Frequent references are made to the House as a haus tambaran, a cult house (see Harding and Lawrence 1971, pp. 181–2). This ignorance of the House of Assembly is paralleled by the villagers' very weak perception of themselves as members of the nation of Papua New Guinea.

The Mabuso Open electorate covers a much larger population than any traditional political unit, 16,470 enrolled voters in 1968 (Papua New Guinea 1968a, Table 1), and in fact includes several local government council areas. With four other Open electorates it comprises the Madang Regional electorate, with an enrolled voting population of 92,144 (Papua New Guinea 1968a, Table 1A). Although these two groupings are intermediate between the

---

[1] For more up-to-date information on most topics in this section see Postscript 1972.

villagers and the House of Assembly, they are not bases for corporate action. There is however some appreciation that the M.H.A.s represent wide areas, and a few councillors are able to consider election tactics in terms of area votes. Furthermore, as I shall argue below, the location of electoral boundaries has considerable political significance in Madang, and the public was keenly interested in this subject in 1968. The dual electorate structure appears to have been important only during the 1968 election campaigns, when Regional and Open candidates formed teams for mutual assistance.

A complicating factor in the national elections in Madang has been that in both 1964 and 1968 Yali was an unsuccessful candidate in the adjacent Rai Coast Open electorate. Despite the fact that he was not standing in their electorate, many Madangs voted for him, their votes being counted as informal. One *lo bos* explained to me: 'In the elections we were told to vote for the man who could give us what we wanted. So we voted for the Old Father [Yali].' The total proportion of informal votes in 1964 in Madang Open was 18·3 per cent (Hughes and van der Veur 1965, p. 420) and in 1968, in what became Mabuso Open, 13·0 per cent (Harding and Lawrence 1971, p. 195). Harding and Lawrence estimate that about 11·3 per cent of the 1968 votes were cast for Yali (1971, p. 195).

It appears that in both elections the underlying issue has been economic development, the primary choice being between development in Western terms on the one hand and the millennial hopes of the cargo cultists on the other (Harding and Lawrence 1971, p. 199). In these terms in 1968 Madangs saw their two local candidates from Ambenob Council, Angmai (Riwo) and Bato (Panim) together with Garrett in the Regional as against cargo, and Yali and a Regional candidate called Whitaker as in favour of it. I do not discuss the other candidates from further afield who received a negligible proportion of the votes in the area under study. In fact Whitaker was officially teamed with Bato, while Angmai alone was Garrett's running-mate. However Whitaker publicly proclaimed his friendship with Yali for political reasons, and probably without full cognizance of the forces he was dealing with. Far from attracting votes, this manoeuvre cost him those of the majority in the electorate who oppose Yali. Furthermore it placed his running-mate, Bato, an outspoken opponent of Yali, in an anomalous and embarrassing position and cost him votes too.

If one choice was between Angmai/Bato/Garrett and Yali/ Whitaker, another choice for the opponents of Yali was between Angmai and Bato. Since Whitaker's alliance with Yali was taken with a pinch of salt by some of Yali's opponents, a few voters did decide between Garrett and Whitaker on other grounds. It appears that voters weighed up the experience, skills and interests of the men and voted accordingly. Angmai and Garrett stressed large-scale district-level development plans, while Bato and Whitaker advocated village improvements (Harding and Lawrence 1971, pp. 173–7). But from my own fieldwork it appears that it was more the reputation and the life-styles of candidates which impressed voters. Angmai, a young man, has a name for being progressive in economic matters through his association with the cooperative movement, the Stevedores Branch of Madang Workers' Association and his own cocoa plantation. He is described as *man bilong bisnis*, a man with commercial know-how. Informants felt that because of this he would be a good man to *gerapim Distrik bilong yumi*, to help develop our District. Arguments for Bato included his experience with the Land Titles Commission and his appreciation of the importance of the traditional land tenure system. Some people voted against Bato because he had been unsuccessful in 1964, or because they wanted an Ambenob M.H.A. and did not want to split the council area vote.

For Ambenob Council elections I argued that local and particularly village interests were dominant. In national elections too on a large scale voters prefer a candidate from their own general area (e.g. Ambenob) rather than a more distant one. Thus 83 per cent of all votes in the three boxes in which among others the villages under study voted were for either Angmai or Bato.[1] Similarly, on a narrower scale, Bato received 60 per cent of all votes in the box which circulated in the villages nearest to his own. However, these figures by no means indicate a unanimous commitment to the local man. When we look at individual villages we find in contrast to the council elections that even in Panim itself everyone did not vote the same way. Indeed several senior men in interviews deplored this lack of unanimity. They

[1] Figures taken from Lawrence (no date) on the ballot box breakdowns.

said they would have preferred a village meeting to have decided on a village vote.

This difference between elections for local and national government can be attributed to a number of factors. In the perceived election choice between Yali and his opponents the decision taken reflected pre-existing lines of support for and hostility to Yali. As can be seen from Table 2, such support would have given Yali a block vote from only one (the smallest) of the 17 villages. In 11 other villages, some would have voted for and some against him. In the remaining five villages, and among non-cultists generally, there remains the question why people did not vote unanimously for either Angmai or Bato. The educational campaign that preceded the election certainly emphasized that every man should decide for himself, but this is equally true of council elections, where pre-arranged village voting is a pattern. Earlier in this chapter I showed how people see the role of councillor as one of village leadership, and in some respects as a continuation of traditional leadership. This would be what D. T. Hughes (1969, p. 38) has described for Ponape in the Eastern Caroline Islands as a 'substituting' role. In contrast, people do not see the role of M.H.A. in terms of traditional patterns or conflicts because it is of larger scale; it is in Hughes' terminology an 'added' leadership role. Such an analysis accords well with voters' stated reasons for preferring Angmai or Bato. They were not looking for a wise village elder type, but for someone who could attract economic development to the area.

The House of Assembly (particularly through the Open electorates where no educational qualification is required) has offered village people a new kind of career and an additional avenue of political advancement. The position of M.H.A. carries a salary larger than most Madangs have ever earned, extensive travel opportunities, prestige and valuable experience. Voters can bring very little influence to bear on the M.H.A. to represent their interests and tell them what is happening, at least until the next election. In Papua New Guinea, with its poor communications system and limited funds for electoral education, the responsibility of the M.H.A. to report back to his constituents is seen as very important. The criticisms I heard of M.H.A.s were that they failed to tell voters what they were doing (a difficult task in view of the geographical extent of the electorates and absence of motor roads) and were feathering their own nests at the nation's expense. At the time of fieldwork neither of the Madang M.H.A.s appeared to have greatly impressed his voters with his performance, despite the fact that at least the Open electorate member attended council meetings and held public meetings quite frequently in the area under study.

6

Cult and Church

In terms of formal structure the Yali movement has only one intermediate level between the individual and the whole organization, namely the village. Cult members within a single village usually have their own appointed *lo bos*, hold regular meetings on Tuesdays and are jointly responsible for assembling financial contributions. But since the cult is a minority movement embracing only slightly over one-third of Madang adult men resident in the Sub-District (see Table 2), one rarely finds a village in which all members are cultists. In fact Yahil is the only one. In the others the proportion of Yali supporters ranges from none in five villages (Foran, Haidurem, Mis, Mukuru and Nobanob) to 92 per cent in Mirkuk and 88 per cent in Kesup. Whether a village can be an independent unit in the movement depends on the number of supporters. Where as in Barahaim there are only a few members they may travel to a nearby village for meetings (in this case Korog) and be responsible to a *lo bos* from outside their own village.

Of those who do not support Yali, all Christians and an indeterminate number of those who neither attend church nor support Yali are actively hostile to him. A higher proportion of this latter category are hostile to Yali in villages such as Korog, Mirkuk and Urugan, where cultists form a large majority. Elsewhere (as in Mis and Panim) men who neither attend church nor support Yali may belong to the growing number of professed agnostics who reject Christianity but refrain from espousing any other creed. I am not aware of any men who profess an exceptional interest in pagan religious beliefs and reject both Yali *and* Christianity. The division into supporters and opponents of Yali changes slightly over time. In the late 1940s support for Yali was at its peak while since then numbers have declined. There have been one or two very prominent defectors. For example, a Lutheran headman at Foran who died in 1968 had been in his time both a leader at a Yali camp and later an outspoken opponent of Yali. In general, however, there has been considerable continuity of leadership, and, of course, of ideology. There has also been a staunch core of Yali supporters through the years, justifying, I believe, my analysis in terms of more or less permanent align-ments.

It is not easy to explain the incidence of individual support for Yali by differences in access to his cult, since all 17 villages have had roughly the same opportunities to become involved (see Table 4 and Chapter 2), and all but one village attended Yali camps immediately after the war. Nor do support and op-position appear to be correlated with traditional groupings. Neither those villages which oppose him nor those where he has some following fall into linguistic groups. It is true that the Austronesian-speaking coastal villages give negligible support to Yali – three out of 548 males in the Sub-District – but their attitude may also reflect a number of other differences between themselves and their inland neighbours. Turning to the village as a unit, we find that even for the Rai Coast and an earlier period (1948–58) when there were fewer alternatives, Lawrence would not argue that there was 100 per cent support for or op-position to Yali in every cargo village (personal communication, 1972, and a clarification of his position in 1964, pp. 188, 198–9). In Madang, although in five villages there are no Yali supporters and in one other support is unanimous, the majority of villages (11) are divided. Survey III indicates that clan allegiance alone is not a sufficient explanation of individual attitudes. Table 11 shows that in the villages where Yali has some support most clans are in some way divided internally. If we exclude the group who neither support Yali nor the church because some of them are fence-sitters on the Yali issue, we find that 25 clans are united and 22 are divided. This kind of analysis is certainly one that suggests itself to Madangs. Informants often noticed whether a clan was united or divided over Yali and mentioned this in discussion.

Another possible explanation is that the family and personal network of kin are significant for cult allegiance. Unfortunately the figures available on this matter from Survey II are rather limited, partly because a large number of sample members did

Table 11. The significance of the clan for affiliation (for all villages containing supporters of Yali excepting Yahil where 100% are in favour of him)

Village	Undivided clans				Divided clans					Excluded	Total
	Christian	Yali	Neither	All	Christian & Yali	Christian & neither	Yali & neither	All 3	All		
Barahaim	1	—	2	3	—	1	2	1	4	—	7
Butelkud	1	—	1	2	2	1	—	1	4	1	7
Kamba	—	1	—	1	4	—	1	3	8	—	9
Kauris	2	1	—	3	1	1	—	1	3	1	7
Kesup	—	3	—	3	1	—	—	—	1	—	4
Korog	—	—	—	—	1	—	1	3	5	1	6
Mirkuk	—	7	1	8	—	—	—	—	—	4	12
Opi	—	2	—	2	—	1	—	1	2	1	5
Panim	—	—	—	—	—	1	2	2	5	—	5
Silabob	4	—	—	4	—	—	1	1	2	1	7
Urugan	—	3	—	3	—	1	—	—	1	3	7
Totals	8	17	4	29	9	6	7	13	35	12	76

Notes: 1. Clans are excluded if they have only one adult male member, only one resident member or only one member whose affiliation is known

2. The table excludes all males resident away from their home village, since clan pressures might be supposed to be less effective in such cases.

not have relatives in all categories. Those which are available are given in Table 12. In this table, the total number of informants is different in some cases from the sum of the other two columns, since an informant may have had relatives in one category who both agreed and disagreed with him. The table suggests that the nuclear family is likely to be united on the Yali/church/'neither' issue. On a hypothesis of randomness we would expect Christians to have only 49 per cent, cultists 34 per cent and 'neithers' 15 per cent of relatives in agreement with them. However, 52 out of

Table 12. Comparison of sample members' allegiance with that of their true relatives

Category of relationship	At least one relative agrees with ego in terms of allegiance to Yali, church or 'neither'	disagrees	Total no. informants
Fa or adopting Fa	31	10	41
FaSis	8	3	11
FaSisSo	12	8	17
MoBro	23	12	34
MoBroSo	28	14	39
Wi	52	5	57
WiFa	8	10	18
WiBro	31	16	42
SisHus	19	8	24
So	16	2	18
	not divided	divided	
Group of brothers	33	7	40

57 sample members said that their wives agreed with them, 31 out of 41 their fathers and 16 out of 18 their adult sons. These latter two sets of figures are recorded separately, since sons may be better informed about their fathers' views than fathers about their sons'.

In Kauris village only two sons are not in agreement with their fathers; their cases are discussed here to illustrate some of the other variables involved. Y., aged 35 in 1969, is a single man and lives alone near his true father in a small house, in which he has a trade store. He is highly educated for his age group (to Standard IV) and worked away from home in Madang Town for about

10 years before returning in 1969. His last job was as a receptionist at Madang General Hospital, his duties involving mainly handling telephone and personal enquiries. For this work he used both English and Pidgin. Y.'s true father's sister is married to one of the *lo bos* at Korog. His father is one of the most ardent supporters of Yali in his own village, and also gave hospitality to Yakob on his first visit. He has considerable knowledge of traditional magic, particularly of a beneficent kind. Y., however, does not support Yali nor pay taxes to him, he argues with his father in private and announces in public that he has no time for Yali. He is a rather quiet man, but his closest relationships seems to be with two of his sisters' husbands (both Christian) and the councillor's Christian sons. Y. himself, although baptized and confirmed, has no wish to be known as a Christian.

The second exceptional man in Kauris is D. He is 27, married to a Christian, and lives in a hamlet with an older brother and his family (pro-Yali), his father, mother, unmarried sister and father's mother (all pro-Yali). In the settlement there is a traditional-style house, which is used for meetings of the Yali community; here his father has a Yali table and flowers. D.'s father is very outspoken in his support for Yali and told me (as mentioned earlier) that he would be buried with Yali's picture on his breast. D. himself, on the other hand, is a practising Lutheran. He has not been continuously under the care of his father. As a baby he was given in adoption to his father's adopted clan brother, M., and his wife S., who were childless. In 1959 M. died, and, since he had no clan land in his own name, D. was taken back at 17 by his true father. S. continues to live with D., her only child, true or adopted, in the village. M. and S. had both been deeply involved with the Lutheran church. Before she was married, S. was a domestic servant in the missionary's house at Nobanob, and after her marriage she travelled with M. on his work as a mission teacher; so D. was brought up in a strong Christian home. It seems that the influence of this, of his foster mother and possibly of her brother, the Lutheran headman in the village, has been decisive in D.'s loyalty to Christianity, even though living so close socially and geographically to those who are opposed to it.

Other qualitative data also support the figures on the significance of the family. In many cases it is clear that women have changed their allegiance on marriage to match their husbands'. Similarly a change of heart on the husband's part is usually accompanied by a parallel change on the wife's. There are only a few cases in which one spouse is pro-Yali and the other adamantly Christian. One such instance known personally to me involves the son of an ardent Yali supporter and the daughter of an equally ardent Christian. There is considerable friction between husband and wife, and the children are alternately dedicated to Christianity and Yali (the first one, a girl, followed her father). It is my impression that the younger he is, the more likely a man is to follow his father's lead, at least in public. This impression draws some support from Table 12, in which 16 out of 18 men said their adult sons agreed with them, but only 31 out of 41 said their fathers did. Looking at each faction in turn, the figures do perhaps suggest that unanimity within the nuclear family may be more marked among cultists than Christians. For the wider kinship and affinal network the figures are too small to be conclusive. Probably only figures for the wife's brother suggest that this relationship might be significant for cult allegiance.

It can also be argued for some villages that the dominance of particular leaders has influenced villagers' positions on the Yali issue. For example Mis even abstained from attending a Yali camp under pressure from its dominant and sceptical *luluai*. In Kamba too the mass reconversion to Yali was led and largely stimulated by a very popular, respected and persuasive leader. But elsewhere (for example in Kauris and Panim) otherwise prominent men cannot carry their villages with them. In general then it is not possible to accord priority to any one of the elements of traditional social structure discussed here, although all have contributed in part to the present pattern.

There also appears to be a more modern dimension to the pattern of cult incidence. The introduction of schools, medical facilities and roads, particularly in the eastern part of the area under study, appears to be roughly correlated with a lower incidence of cultism. Thus Foran, Haidurem, Mis and Nobanob (where there are no Yali followers) have benefited from a disproportionate amount of mission and government expenditure. This is also true to a lesser extent of more inland Mukuru. The Lutheran Mission owns land traditionally belonging to both Nobanob and Haidurem and has established stations, an aid post, a saw mill and schools on it. Mis had the first Administration village primary school in the District, and Foran is the nearest of all to town and its amenities. From Nobanob, Mis and Foran villagers are able to commute daily to work in town. Men from these villages are probably among the best educated in Madang, and so are more employable and earn better rates. My market survey shows that those who have farther to walk to motor roads tend to attend Madang market less frequently to sell their produce. The correlation between cult and isolation would be more clearly seen if we were to extend our observations beyond the 17 villages under study. Coastwards the Austronesian-speaking villages give negligible support to Yali, while farther inland towards Gal, Matepi and Baimak we find very large proportions of cultists.

Within villages such factors are relatively constant. Divisions within villages appear to have been made possible by various social changes: the cessation of warfare, the destruction of the men's cult and the loss of the magic which made men and clans interdependent. Simultaneously economic and social differentiation has increased. My field data suggest that not only is this differentiation a precondition for the development of divisions within the village, it may also help to explain where they fall. In the first place there are educational differences correlated with the Yali/Christian division. Only 33 per cent of Christians are illiterate, as opposed to 69 per cent of cultists (Survey II), and only 7 per cent of cultists have any kind of post-primary education in contrast with 26 per cent of Christians (figures significant at the 90 per cent level only). It might be expected that age would be related to education and hence to cult allegiance, but my figures from Survey II are not conclusive on this question. It is possible that outsiders overestimate the age variable in discussion of cults in Madang. The young people who live near home are strongly influenced by their parents, especially in what they are prepared to say in public. Two of the five student sample members interviewed at Tusbab High School in Madang Town declared themselves in favour of Yali, and a third said he supported Yali in the village and went to church when away. This young man said he was genuinely confused about the value of Yali's teachings. I had deliberately chosen to meet these students away from home and out of earshot of their fathers, and yet they still maintained

their convictions about Yali. The more education young people
have, the more doubts about Yali they are likely to feel, but it
appears that few will give public expression to such doubts until
they have gained considerable independence from their homes.
The case of a youngish man in Kauris who has displayed such
independence has already been given. Some young Madangs
known to me in Madang Town, Lae and Port Moresby express
opposition to their fathers' support for Yali (including the son
of one and the daughter of another *lo bos*). However, what matters
here is that few young people at home are prepared to make a

Table 13. Coconut holdings and support for Yali of males
resident in own villages

	Supporters of Yali	Christians	'Neither'
Average no. palms per man	32·2	112	32·9
Percentage growers in each group	21·8	51·1	13·8
Average no. palms per plantation	149	244	299

Sources: Survey III (for affiliations) and D.A.S.F., Project Areas 6 and 7 (for
individual holdings).

Notes: 1. These figures are based not on a sample, but on all men whose
affiliation was known.

2. The table covers all villages where there was support for Yali, except Opi
and Urugan for which no D.A.S.F. figures were available.

public statement on their doubts about Yali if their father supports
him, or to take any political action in terms of these doubts.

There also appears to be a correlation between support for
Yali and low economic status. Only one-third of Yali supporters
own pass books, compared with 66 per cent of Christians (Survey
II). Yali supporters are also less likely to take part in cash cropping,
and those who do so display less initiative and energy than
Christians. My evidence for this comes from a comparison of all
coconut and cocoa holdings with alignments on the church/cult
issue. Table 13 shows that in the villages where Yali has some
support the average number of coconut palms owned by cultists
is 32, while for Christians the same figure is nearly four times as
large, namely 112. These figures reflect both a lower proportion
of growers in the cultist population and smaller plantations on

average among those who have planted. Similarly, although to a lesser extent, Table 14 shows that Christians outdo Yali supporters in cocoa growing. Although the proportion of cocoa growers is roughly the same among Christians and cultists, Christians who plant at all appear to plant more trees. Thus the difference between cultists and Christians is more marked in coconut than in cocoa holdings. One reason is that coconuts are a more labour-intensive crop taking a longer time to yield any income and so demand greater commitment to commercial production. Moreover no encouragement was offered for coconut

Table 14. Cocoa holdings and support for Yali of males
resident in own villages

	Supporters of Yali	Christians	'Neither'
Average no. trees per man	129	256	106
Percentage growers in each group	34·6	39·2	37·9
Average no. trees per plantation	372	565	380

Sources: As for Table 13, plus records for 33 of the 135 growers taken from D.A.S.F., File 'Councillor Kaut. Agriculture Committee'.

Notes: 1. See Table 13.
2. The table covers all villages where there was support for Yali.

planting comparable to that given by the Ambenob Cocoa Project, which appealed to Christians and cultists alike.

The correlation of high participation in cash cropping with opposition to Yali does not hold good for the five unanimously anti-Yali villages. Tables 15 and 16 show that in these villages Christians own about one-third as many coconut palms and one-fifth as many cocoa trees as their counterparts elsewhere, and that the level of cash cropping is generally low. It may be that here land alienation has been a significant factor in reducing ability and willingness to grow tree crops. Furthermore, with a long history of close and not entirely amicable contact with Administration and expatriates, there is some resistance in these villages to new D.A.S.F. schemes. As one Mis informant told me, 'We planted cocoa and coffee but it didn't bring us much money. So we said "they [the agricultural officers] too are just lying".'

For these villages it seems that it is education, strong mission influence, the provision of amenities and their accessibility to Madang Town, enabling many of them to be wage earners, which have been decisive in their rejection of Yali.

These correlations between cultism and other variables raise questions of cause and effect; for example, were people literate before becoming Christians or cultists? It should be remembered that all pre-war education was given in church schools, and that

Table 15. Coconut holdings in villages unanimously opposed to Yali (excepting Foran, for which no D.A.S.F. figures were available)

	Christians	'Neither'	Both
Average no. palms per man	35·0	136	77·6
Percentage growers in each group	17·3	41·7	18·6
Average no. palms per plantation	203	328	219

Sources: As for Table 13.

Table 16. Cocoa plantings in villages unanimously opposed to Yali (excepting Mukuru, for which no D.A.S.F. figures were available)

	Christians	'Neither'	Both
Average no. trees per man	54·7	85·3	56·6
Percentage growers in each group	16·3	30·8	17·2
Average no. trees per plantation	336	277	329

Sources: As for Table 14, with records for 4 of the 36 growers taken from the alternative source.

most people had been baptized by one mission or another in that period. Hence one could not say that better educated adults chose to become Christians. The figures suggest rather that education has at the very least been a deterrent to conversion to Yali, and that those who were more prone to support him after the war were the effectively uneducated. Cause and effect are interwoven too in the economic data. It is true that once involved in the cult people may be discouraged from planting new cash crops or fully exploiting the ones they have. But it seems reasonable to conclude that in many cases comparatively low economic status existed prior to the decision to support Yali or that the attitudes (including cargo thinking) which had previously influenced decisions about cash cropping were further evidenced in views on Yali. After 1950 most of Yali's support went underground or was lost. It has only been in the 1960s that overt support has grown again. Most of the tree crops (especially coconuts) which are at present producing income for their owners must have been planted *before* the second upsurge of support for Yali.

Foreigners resident in Madang occasionally take part in Yali's movement. Individual affines living in a village may follow the lead of their hosts. Thus one man from the Northern District took a keen interest in Yali activities through his father-in-law. Labourers and members of discrete settlements are less likely to be involved in the cult because of their infrequent contact with local villagers, and because they often come from distant areas where there is no sympathy for or knowledge of Yali's activities. An exception is a settlement of people from villages immediately across the Gogol River, an area with a long history of support for Yali. These people have continued their allegiance in their new surroundings and have two subsidiary leaders (not quite *lo bos*) of their own, who contact the main movement through the *lo bos* at Kesup. They operate as an independent unit in the Yali movement and collected a typical village contribution of $10 in 1968.

The distribution of Yali's officials in the Madang villages is shown in Table 17. Of the 'other officials' shown, the itinerant secretary travels widely with news and recent instructions from Yali, the 'soldier' is an ex-policeman whose position dates from camp days and involves him in no activities, the Mirkuk man (resident in Yahil) spends about half his time as a labourer for Yali on the Rai Coast, and the lower level village leader insists that he is not a *lo bos*, although his role appears very similar.

The prime quality which all 10 *lo bos* have in common, and which they probably possessed before their official appointment, is their extraordinary enthusiasm for their leader. On average they were between 45 and 50 years old in 1969. They fall into two distinct groups: the seniors were appointed in the early days of the camps, the juniors more recently, after the upsurge of support for Yali in the 1960s. The former, the old *lo bos* of Korog and Kesup, enjoy considerable prestige and influence in their

I

dealings with Yali and other *lo bos*. At least 6 of the 10 canno[t] read or write (one *lo bos* was not interviewed personally) an[d] none of them speaks English. Six have cocoa planted, three coco-nuts and one coffee. Three have no cash crops, but one of thes[e] works as a casual stevedore. Four had previously occupie[d] positions as medical assistant, policeman, councillor and *komit[i]* respectively. My general impression from talking to these an[d]

Table 17. Yali officials (1969) in the villages where he has support

Village	No. of adult men for Yali	No. of lo bos	Year of appointment	Other officials
Barahaim	6	—	—	—
Butelkud	9	1	1969	—
Kamba	57	1	1967	—
Kauris	18	1	1968	itinerant secretary
Kesup	37	2	both 1947	—
Korog	28	2	both 1947	'soldier'
Mirkuk	37	1	1965	plantation hand
Opi	13	—	—	lower level villag[e] leader
Panim	5	1	1968	—
Silabob	2	—	—	—
Urugan	22	1	?	—
Yahil	10	—	—	—
Totals	244	10		

other *lo bos* is that they do not constitute an élite in the same way as the councillors. It could indeed be argued that they need to b[e] less well educated than the majority even of their own follower[s] to be as involved in Yali's movement as they are. The ex-schoolteacher *lo bos* in Kamba would be an exception, as indeed are Kamba people as a whole. My feeling is that their support for Yali is to a certain extent a matter of convenience rather than principle. They are using cargo cult as a form of protest against authority (see also the Kamba tax courts in Chapter 5). Since they do not represent villagers in any western-type institutions, there is no reason why the *lo bos* should be able to cope with such institutions. Their abilities lie in more traditional spheres – exchanges, oratory and wisdom in decision-making.

The role expectations for a *lo bos* are much less well-defined than for a councillor. He should instruct villagers in Yali's latest teachings, hold Tuesday meetings and collect the various financial contributions. Beyond that he can make what he likes of his position. Certain *lo bos* (especially the senior ones) have considerable influence outside their own villages; they often have rights, such as that of administering the Yali baptism, which give them priority over others. Such influence would certainly be one of the advantages of being a *lo bos*. The other main one is that, given the cultist's conceptual framework, the *lo bos* hopes that his labours will secure him a major share in the anticipated riches and power of the millenium. *Lo bos* are able to make very little out of their position in terms of supporting other specific leadership roles they may occupy (e.g. Parents and Citizens' Association chairman). However, their general influence in the village may subsidize and in turn enhance their being *lo bos*. I do not think the *lo bos* syphon off for their own use much of the money they collect; they are too afraid of Yali's anger.

The *lo bos* certainly has his problems as the official representative of a persecuted minority. He collects substantial funds but promises returns of a very insubstantial nature; hence he is subject to popular pressure for more tangible results. It is undoubtedly this pressure as well as their own enthusiasm which has encouraged *lo bos* to urge Yali to stand in national elections, to declare him 'king', and to foretell that he would bring 'independence' on 1 August 1969. It is clear to me that Yali took the original initiative in none of these events. On the kingship question he himself told me '*ol lo bos yet ol i makim mi*' (it was the *lo bos* themselves who appointed me). On 'independence' he said, 'I never started this talk. It's all the *lo bos*' idea. It's not mine. I have told them off . . . How can we have self-government? Where are our ships, where are our guns?' And on the activities of the *lo bos* in general, Yali told me, 'I don't tell people to do things. They do it anyway. If I didn't fall in with them, they'd be ashamed and cross with me.'

Another feature of the Yali movement is the network of kinship and affinal ties linking the various leaders. Six of the 10 are known to me to be related to other Yali officials. One of the Korog *lo bos*, for example, is married to a sister of the Butelkud *lo bos*. A more complex chain of interrelationships involving officials and prominent supporters in Gal, Opi, Korog, Kauris and Kesup is illustrated in Figure 1. In most cases these ties were created *before* the appointment of at least one of the parties involved. The close contact between affines in Madang exposes each to all the enthusiasms of the other. *Lo bos* seem in several cases to have been appointed at the instance of the village, with Yali's consent, when they were already informal leaders in the movement. A man with an affine already heavily committed would have the opportunity to hear news, to be an unofficial messenger and to visit Sor with an introduction from someone

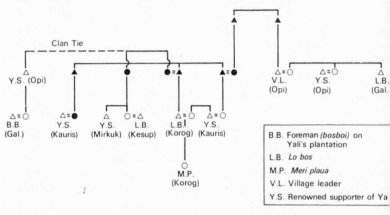

Fig. 1. The network of personal ties between Yali supporters and officials in a few Madang villages

already in Yali's confidence. These personal ties are an important element in the united front which the *lo bos* present to the outside world, and are channels for the close inter-village communication which characterizes the movement. The Ambenob councillors are not linked in the same way; they live at some distance from each other, whereas marriages as we have seen are most common between adjacent and nearby villages. Moreover, the role of councillor is defined more clearly and requires qualities found only in a few men. The role of *lo bos* demands first and foremost loyalty and enthusiasm. Nevertheless many *lo bos* are important, if not the most important and influential, men in their villages (see Chapter 7). A *lo bos* who dies may be succeeded by his son, but perhaps the most noticeable influence of the family is in the recruitment of *meri plaua*. These are always the daughters of

Yali supporters and very frequently of *lo bos*: one such case is illustrated in Figure 1.

There is relatively little political conflict within Yali's movement, for a number of reasons. As with the church, the meetings, discussions and speeches of the cultists are largely directed to their own ritual welfare and the promotion of types of behaviour considered likely to bring about *gutpela lo*. Villages are not competing for scarce resources or in dispute over contributions. Although the benefits expected from the movement are at present intangible and unquantifiable, abundance is expected in the future. Contributions are fairly flexible (despite the $10 p.a. per village 'rule'), it being generally held that your share in the future is somehow related to your current contributions. There may sometimes be wrangling over individual contributions to a village's donation to Yali, though I have no evidence of this. Certainly the *lo bos* can recall accurately the sums received. Other reasons why there is little internal conflict are that the cultists are a threatened minority in a largely hostile community and that their organization is undemocratic by the standards of Ambenob Council and the Lutheran church. The movement is dominated by Yali (who is considerably influenced by local leaders), but the mass of followers are content to obey its rules and receive what scraps of information filter through to them. In fact attempts to learn what are supposed to be the cult's secrets are one of the few forms of rivalry among leaders.

I have seldom observed any evidence of conflict, at least at a local level. There was however a clear disagreement over Yakob's cult. In 1968 Yali supporters in some villages, such as Korog and Opi, refused to support Yakob, while in others, such as Kauris, they did so enthusiastically. A Korog *lo bos* justified his disapproval of Yakob to me by alleging that Yakob was secretly hostile to Yali, but he also had serious doubts about Yakob's ability to produce the goods. Even in this case the disagreement did not appear to result in hostile action, merely in a shrug of the shoulders and a '*samting bilong ol, mipela yet i no laik*' (that's their affair, we ourselves don't want to join).

THE CHURCH

Participation in E.L.C.O.N.G. involves various types of corporate activity. The Lutheran tradition includes family worship, and every household is expected to gather daily or even twice daily for prayers, though by no means all do. Sometimes two or more families meet for such worship. One prominent man was usually joined by his wife, his married son and daughter-in-law, their children and his own brother and his family.

Lutheran missionaries as did German administrators before them selected the village as the basic unit of their formal hierarchy, and in many established schools and churches. Today the village survives in the church structure, but with an important modification of the original mission intention, namely that not all the village is involved in church activities. Only slightly under half of the adult men in Madang today consider themselves as practising Christians (see Table 2); hence the Christian community within a village is by no means coterminous with the village as a whole. In some cases nearly all members are Christians (e.g. Haidurem and Nobanob); in others a sizeable proportion (e.g. Butelkud and Kauris); in such villages as Barahaim, Korog and Opi Christians are a small minority, and in still others there are none at all (e.g. Mirkuk and Yahil). In only the first two cases can the Christians in a single village be said to act as an independent unit. In Barahaim, Korog and Opi there are no church buildings, and no regular Sunday worship, and Christians from these villages sometimes travel to Kauris or Foran on Sundays.

In three villages, Butelkud, Mukuru and Panim, the Christian community is further divided between two denominations (Lutherans and Roman Catholics in Butelkud and Mukuru, Lutherans and Seventh Day Adventists in Panim). Each section worships by itself and is separately organized and integrated into a different extra-village power structure. The village worshipping community today also includes foreigners. The Wanuma labourers are keen Lutherans and attend whatever forms of worship are offered by the Lutherans in the villages where they are employed. Some inhabitants of discrete settlements attend church services in the villages, especially where as in Mis there is a large building exclusively used for that purpose. But these outsiders rarely play an important part in leadership or decision-making in the Christian community.

Regular church services provide an opportunity for more than ritual. By the time everyone has gathered, worshipped, stood around talking afterwards and gone home, the process has usually taken a full morning and has involved considerable informal contact between worshippers. Often a Sunday school is organized to coincide with the church service. Village Christians also jointly own church buildings which they have probably worked together to erect. These may include a pastor's house and Sunday school building as well as the church itself. Cemeteries however are village, not Christian property, and are used, though with different rituals, by all village members. The Christian community in a village is responsible for raising funds for various church activities (such as primary schools, pastors' salaries, the District Bible School etc.), and for providing assistance in kind on different occasions. Thus in 1968 the surrounding villages helped to provide food for delegates to the District Conference held in Siar village.

The Christian community, either as a group or through its officials, exercises certain forms of moral control. One Lutheran told me, 'A congregation should take responsibility for all marriages. We can't annul them, just help to put them right.' Where there is serious trouble in a marriage, the headman or pastor may advise the couple privately, or a meeting may be held to censure one partner or pray for guidance. In cases of adultery an unrepentant partner is denied Holy Communion. Christians may also assemble for prayers over special problems such as serious illness or, as happens in one village, when the cargo cultists become ultra-active. The village may be jointly responsible for hospitality to congregational or even circuit and District assemblies; for example women's retreats rotate between the villages of a congregation.

The village elects its own Lutheran headman. He is responsible *to* the villagers as well as *for* them, and may as one pastor told me be reported to a pastor or even the circuit council if unsatisfactory. The Lutheran emphasis on family life, and the traditional Madang political and ritual differences between men and women, have led to a fairly marked differentiation of the sexes in church affairs, but not to a neglect of women. At services men and women sit on opposite sides of the church. Headmen, evangelists and pastors are all men, but the women have their own 'women's work', which involves them in separate spiritual retreats (day-long meetings for prayers, hymns and talks), Sunday schools and the provision of food for certain occasions. The women have their own elected leaders at village, congregational and circuit level. Their importance is also recognized in the requirement that they attend with their husbands at pastors' refresher courses. Indeed their status has been advanced more in church work than elsewhere. With a competent and enthusiastic female at its head, the women's work can even become one of the dominant elements in a village's Christian life. Thus at Foran there is an impressive building for women's work but no church. The activities of the Lutheran Youth League bring together young people from different villages in religious meetings, fund-raising activities and semi-social gatherings. These groups too have elected leaders at different levels.

Ordinary rank-and-file Christians as well as officials from different villages have many reasons to meet one another. Holy Communion is celebrated by the pastor at only one or two villages in a congregation. People from the others travel to preparatory classes and to the actual service. Observers who are not officials often attend circuit and District conferences. There were 14 people from Nobanob congregation at the circuit conference at Fulumu from 28 May to 2 June 1968. The holding of conferences in different locations also gives an opportunity for members of the host village to meet delegates informally. School events and graduation days bring villagers together, as do large-scale events in town such as the inauguration of the Pidgin English New Testament. Communications are facilitated in these gatherings by the use of Pidgin or one of several languages officially used by the Lutheran mission at one time or another.

Although the common view is that a man's religion is his own affair (*laik bilong man*), there is a certain amount of friction between different denominations. There is an area of strong Roman Catholic influence to the north of that under study. Butelkud and Mukuru are on the boundary, so to speak. One Lutheran informant said, 'Before there was a bit of friction. Now there isn't. Well, perhaps there's a little – over work and church attendance, but that's all.' An example of conflict is the complaint in the Lutherans' 1958 Amele Circuit report (E.L.C.O.N.G. 1958) that Roman Catholics were baptizing children of unbaptized parents. Another area of difficulty is intermarriage. The general feeling is that a woman should be instructed in her husband's religion, but there is some official discouragement of marriage outside the church.

At church meetings many discussions and speeches are directed
to the spiritual welfare of the community and promotion of the
gospel outside it. Church activity is regarded as having value in
itself, regardless of material benefits or costs. Some issues however
arouse a certain amount of competition and conflict, particularly
as with Ambenob Council between villages as interest groups.
There is debate on the amount of contributions and on the allocation of funds controlled at an inter-village level. Some people
object to the expenditure of time, labour and food involved in
holding conferences. It was only after several weeks of wrangling
that the Nobanob-Wagi congregation agreed to contribute to
the food supplies for the District Conference at Siar. As with
Ambenob Council, there is considerable competition to attract
expenditure on mission aid posts and schools for one's own
village or area.

The church provides a full-time career for pastors, teachers and
evangelists, and an opportunity for part-time but sometimes
extremely influential leadership for headmen, circuit council
members etc. This used probably to be a much more important
avenue of social mobility than it is today, when there are government schools and numerous secular career opportunities in the
towns. Church officials in villages where Christians are in a
minority wield much less influence in their village as a whole
than those where there is a high proportion of Christians. In
Nobanob, an almost entirely Christian village, an old Lutheran
headman is probably the most influential person of all.

PART III
THE POLITICAL SCENE

7

The Leaders

FORMAL LEADERSHIP

The structure within which officials operate today differs in many respects from the traditional village parish system. Madang is now ultimately controlled from Canberra, even though an increasing number of decisions are being taken in the House of Assembly in Port Moresby. As a result, a large number of events with considerable significance for villagers' lives take place beyond their comprehension and even more certainly beyond their control. Agents of the Administration are near at hand but over these too the villager has no authority. However he may on occasion attempt to manipulate these external power foci to his own benefit in terms of the village political scene. Case 6, if referring to somewhat distant events, clearly illustrates this point:

Case 6. Two wily sons

In the late 1940s B. of K. village was attracted to the widow of another member of his village, and wanted to marry her. Her two sons did not approve of their mother's remarriage, and turned to friends in another village to help them. It was agreed that these friends should report B. and others to the District Office for cargo cult activity and in particular for having sexual intercourse with young girls during cult rituals. It was known that at this time the District Office was out to suppress cults and, as predicted, the office responded to the reports received by having B. arrested, tried, convicted and jailed. The real cause of the trouble never became known to the authorities, but their predictable behaviour was the means by which the two sons achieved their desired end.

There are today in Madang a number of formally discrete authority structures within which people and groups compete for power. Whereas the traditional clan and village were functionally diffuse and were concerned equally with ritual, gardening,

marriage, warfare and disputes, the new institutions are functionally specific. The Madang Workers' Association regulates relations between employers and employees in town, and the
Land Titles Commission is entirely concerned with land matters.
Although the clan and village *tamaniak* survives today, it has
lost many of its traditional functions, and is concerned mainly
with the discussion of disputes and misdemeanours. But in
practice it may coincide with other meetings, such as those
convened by a councillor, and may on occasion discuss such
matters as economic development. The villagers are not always
clear about the divisions of jurisdiction. One councillor in a
single meeting both urged a group of foreigners to attend the
church in their host's village and live Christian lives, and exhorted
them to pay their council taxes, keep their paths and roads
clear and build good latrines. Such confusion arises both from the
survival of traditional models in the actors' minds and, probably
more importantly, from the pattern of alliances and hostilities
among participants in the functionally specific institutions (to be
described in Chapter 8). In contrast to the organizations so far
discussed, Yali's movement follows traditional lines much more
closely. It is neither a pagan cult nor an anti-white political
movement nor a mechanism of social control nor an alternative
or partial alternative to cash cropping; but it is simultaneously
all of these. This multiplicity of aims contributes to the persistence
of the cult. Failure in one field need not discredit it in the eyes of
supporters whose other aspirations continue.

These discrete formal structures in Madang are hierarchically
organized in a series of levels of increasing inclusiveness. The
individual council voter belongs first to his village, then his
ward, his area and then the whole Ambenob Council. He is
indirectly represented at the District Conference and at the
Local Government Association of Papua New Guinea. Such
hierarchical organization not only involves the villager in a
much wider political arena than that with which he was traditionally familiar, but also introduces elements of alienation. He is
no longer able to participate directly in or often even to understand the decision-making process at every level. In addition his
political influence, or that of his representative at any particular
level, is restricted by the number of other participants with
whom he is competing.

The individual villager belongs to a number of hierarchies, the higher levels of which in all cases extend beyond the boundaries of his own village. Table 18 indicates both the relative inclusiveness of the intermediate levels and the ultimate level which each hierarchy reaches. Only five of the nine structures extend throughout the nation (all of these sponsored by the national Administration), while four do not even reach the boundaries of the District. In addition the lower multi-village levels are all on different scales. The Open electorate includes several local government councils besides Ambenob, while the boundaries of Amele Circuit are not congruent with those of the L.T.C.'s Avisan Adjudication Area. There is formal provision for the village in only five cases, while the clan fares even less well, being recognized only by the Land Titles Commission and the *tamaniak*.

Since boundaries are drawn differently by different institutions, neighbours may face in the same direction for some hierarchies and in the opposite for others. Thus Nobanob is in a different council ward from Kamba, Kauris, Mis and Silabob, but in the same Lutheran congregation. In some cases there is a relationship between these small multi-village groups and language groups. Both the Lutherans and the council appear to have tried to follow language groupings in their organization of lower-level inter-village units. Thus there is an Austronesian-speaking Bel congregation and a non-Austronesian-speaking Nobanob one. Similarly there is a rough coincidence between council wards and language groups. But there are exceptions. Yahil and Foran are in the same ward as Mirkuk and Panim although they speak two different languages. I have suggested already that inter-village land disputes may be solved most easily where the informal mechanisms provided by affinity supplement the formal machinery. It is possible that the coincidence of wards and congregations with language groups similarly assists inter-village leadership and cooperation; this argument is supported by data in Chapter 5 on the value of affines to a councillor.

Whereas everyone was in theory involved in the traditional activities of village and clan, today the formal composition of lower-level units in different organizations is much more varied, in part because of modes of recruitment. Membership of clan and village for purposes of the Land Titles Commission and

Table 18. Organizational levels of various political structures

Structure	Individual	Clan	Village	Multi-village (smaller than District) 1	2	3	District	Nation
Cooperative	X	—	—	(area)	Madang Cocoa Coop. circuit	—	X	X
E.L.C.O.N.G.	X	—	X	congregation	—	—	X	sub-national church
Land Titles Commission	X	X	X	Adjudication Area	—	—	—	X
Local government	X	—	X	ward	(area)	A.L. G.C.	X	X
Madang Workers' Association	X	—	—	Branch	M.W.A.	—	—	X
National government	X	—	—	Open electorate	—	—	Regional electorate	X
Parents and Citizens' Association	X	—	—	whole P. & C.	—	—	—	—
Tamaniak	X	X	X	—	—	—	—	—
Yali's movement	X	—	X	whole movement	—	—	—	—
		2	5				4	5

tamaniak is ascribed by birth; membership of a council ward or a House of Assembly electorate by birth or residence. Every man or woman is compulsorily and theoretically a member of some ward or electorate except in the most remote areas of the country. But membership of several other organizations is entirely optional, depending on the tastes and interests of the individual. Thus only a cocoa grower would want to join the cooperative, and in fact many choose not to do so. Similarly it is up to each individual whether he attends church, pays taxes to Yali or does neither. Certain organizations – for example the church and the M.W.A. – also have the right to suspend or terminate membership.

Hence all members of a village are not necessarily involved in every institution which is organized at the village level. The Christian community in Kauris encompasses 17 men, while 18 completely different men constitute the Yali group in the village. Because the village as a unit of council administration and the *tamaniak* largely coincide in terms of membership, they are often operationally indistinguishable. For instance, a meeting was held in Kauris on Sunday, 7 July 1968, at which information about council work was followed by a discussion of two disputes. In villages such as Mis and Nobanob, council affairs, disputes and church matters involve almost the same community. One meeting can be used to discuss all three. But in a village where Christians form a smaller proportion of the population, church and council meetings are necessarily separate. Then the councillor has to rely for attendance on the intrinsic attraction of his meeting. Where council and Christian community nearly coincide, the leadership hierarchy of each may reinforce the other and the ideals of one can be used to support the other. A councillor can appeal to the headman to support his decision and claim that it is in consonance with Christian ideals. That this is particularly likely because of political alignments will be apparent in Chapter 8. But in a village where Christians and council voters do not coincide, the councillor in particular is in a weaker position. In order to keep the support of his pagan villagers, he cannot appeal to any but secular authorities for support. A further result of optional membership is that some villages only interact with others in certain spheres. Thus Mirkuk and Yahil, having no Christians, do not interact with the other 15 villages through the Lutheran church, and men from Haidurem, Mis, Mukuru and

K

Nobanob have no occasion to meet other villages in the context of Yali's movement. On the other hand, in that of the Land Titles Commission and Ambenob Council every village in Madang has contact with every other.

Different categories of people participate differently in the nine political structures. Women remain outside several organizations (e.g. the cooperative), while they are at least theoretically involved in others (e.g. the P. and C.'s). But there is often a gap between what women are permitted to do in the villages under study, and the extent to which they do in fact participate. Thus in the 1969 council elections, only 18 per cent of women voters, as opposed to 31 per cent of men, turned out to vote (A.L.G.C., Ward Voting Registers). At Tax Payers', other council and *tamaniak* meetings women if they attend at all usually sit on the outside and rarely speak, except in disputes involving women. To date no women have held office in any of the organizations under discussion except the Lutheran 'women's work'. In Yali's movement and the Lutheran church women have their own discrete sphere of activity and influence. This situation appears to result largely from traditional beliefs and attitudes. As one relatively enlightened male Christian informant told me, 'A woman has no status (*em i no gat nem*). She helps her husband, who does all the fighting and working. We tend to look down on (*rabisim*) women a bit. Half our traditional ideas are still with us.' This is not to deny, however, that some ambitious and talented women enjoy considerable behind-the-scenes influence in village politics.

Participation in several activities depends on place of residence. Those 12 per cent or so of men who live outside the Sub-District have no affiliation with the Madang sections of the Lutheran church or with Yali's movement. Nor are they likely to be members of the Workers' Association or a Madang Parents and Citizens, although they may affiliate with their counterparts (and similarly for the church) elsewhere. However those living nearer home may be involved in the home branch of each of these institutions. In some other organizations a villager absent from Madang can still be affiliated to his home unit. Thus in land matters he remains a legal member of his clan and in the House of Assembly elections he may vote in the electorate either of his residence or of his birth. Foreigners in Madang appear to participate to varying degrees in different political activities. Those living on alienated land are involved only in the M.W.A. and the P. and C.'s, both rather marginal to the main stream of village politics. Affines, labourers and members of discrete settlements take a fuller part in activities such as those of the church, but in general their participation falls far short of that of land-owning Madangs.

As in traditional Madang every official has his own sphere of operation, this being defined in the present situation by the institutional framework within which he operates. In church meetings the headman presides, in local government meetings the councillor. Two illustrations can be given here of the extent to which the role of councillor is specific. One night a major dance rehearsal was organized by the owner of a dance. The councillor arrived late, sat quietly watching, offered no advice and slept through a large part of the night, not being a dancing man himself. But just after dawn, when the practice was over, he sprang into action, calling an impromptu village meeting and haranguing his exhausted fellow villagers about taxes and roads while he had them all conveniently together in one place. Another example of the definition of spheres of authority comes from a conversation with a councillor. He told me that he would not go in his official capacity to a fund-raising party in his own village unless the *papa bilong pati* (the organizer) invited him. He might, however, go as a private citizen.

Villagers perceive functional distinctions between different roles and appear to think it better for one man to do only one job at a time. Informants told me on several occasions '*wanpela man i no ken bungim tupela wok*' (one man must not pile up [lit.] two jobs). This echoes the traditional division of labour between magicians. In keeping with this ethic and in part as a result of it, even relatively small jobs are shared around in some villages. In Kauris only one out of five clans has the same man as Demarcation representative and land leader, and the positions of councillor, *komiti*, Lutheran headman and P. and C. representative are all held by different men. This sharing often has the effect of distributing extra-clan offices between different clans in the traditional pattern, especially where these clans are small. Yet it does not appear that in many villages one clan has monopolized one office over a long period of time. Only in Haidurem was I told that one clan had regularly supplied the Lutheran head-man, while another monopolized the government position of the day, whether *luluai*, *tultul*, *komiti* or councillor.

Everything said so far about the relationship between offices appears to reinforce the distinction between the formal structures. Nevertheless one man may hold several positions at the same time and many hold one after another. Table 19 shows that 11 of the

Table 19. Other offices concurrently held by councillors in February 1969

Office	No. of councillors
Cooperative committee member	2
Deputy Land Titles Commissioner	1
Lutheran headman	4
Lutheran circuit council member	1
Madang Tourist Association committee member	1
Member of the Administrator's Executive Council	1
Member of the House of Assembly	1
P. and C. committee member	3
Stevedore foreman	1
Village pottery business committee member	1
Village tourist committee member	1
Sub-total	11 councillors in 17 jobs
Ex-officio	
District Advisory Council member	1
Local Government Association member	1
Madang Hospital Board member	1
Madang Market trustee	4
Total	14 councillors in 24 jobs

37 councillors hold a total of 17 other positions, apart from those which some of them fill simply because they are councillors. One man occupies a total of five other positions. This pluralism is characteristic of the inter- rather than the intra-village sphere. Only the four men who are Lutheran headmen occupy a village leadership position in addition to that of councillor; the pottery and tourist committee members occupy sub-village-level roles. For the 10 *lo bos* studied there is a similar pattern of duplication.

Two are *komiti*, two P. and C. officials and one a Demarcation representative (a total of four *lo bos*). Among both councillors and *lo bos*, then, it is only a sizeable minority who occupy more than one position.

Duplication of offices arises both because in the inter-village sphere there cannot be the kind of coordination of appointments which occurs within the village and because the occupation of one office may qualify a person in terms of experience and prestige or enable him to manipulate selection mechanisms so that he can successfully compete for another office. Thus, as Lawrence (1970, p. 99) has pointed out, candidates in national elections have frequently been local government councillors (e.g. Angmai and Bato from Ambenob in Mabuso in 1968) and have had to rely on support from councils and thus on their position as councillors.[1] As mentioned earlier, the successful Open candidate in 1968 had held office in the council, a cooperative and the M.W.A., experiences which enabled him to appeal to voters on a number of different grounds. It could also perhaps be argued that there is a shortage of able well-qualified men for the many offices which exist today. People may be faced with the choice of appointing someone incompetent or of giving the job to someone who already has another. Indeed it was stated at a sub-committee meeting at the Lutheran District Conference in 1968 that the church was having difficulty in finding good leaders. I also know several multiple office holders who said (genuinely, I believe) that they would have been happy to step down from at least one of their positions if a willing and competent successor had been to hand.

The nine functionally discrete institutions in Madang are also linked by the movement of officials between them. In the course of his career an individual may move through several positions in different organizations. Thus the M.H.A. had previously held other positions, and the councillors themselves have had a wealth of previous experience in other fields (see Table 9). In fact only 3 of the 37 councillors have neither held any other post previously nor are currently doing so. Of these one has had above-average experience in employment outside the village and another is the son of an ex-*luluai*.

---

[1] This is also a marked pattern at the national level for both candidates and members. See Wolfers 1968/9, p. 14.

INFORMAL LEADERSHIP

Informal leadership is independent of the functionally specific institutions so far discussed, and is by definition restricted geographically. Hence it has not played an important part in the widening political arena in which new officials have begun to operate. Although I by no means equate high status and political influence, I shall begin this section by outlining the various ways in which men gain status. In Madang the traditional ideal of a generous man (*lo man* in Pidgin) continues. Such a man is concerned with two types of distribution, both of which enhance his prestige and both of which are translated into Pidgin as *lo*. On the one hand he gives *oro* (Kamba language), hospitality and small-scale gifts. These are not expected to be returned, and create a reputation for openhandedness. On the other hand he gives *mata* (Kamba language), larger-scale presentations to a particular designated person. As an informant said, '*mata em i gat bek bilong en*', a return is expected for *mata*. When a man dies his son inherits this relationship. Both these activities enhance a man's general prestige, but only the second confers potential for particularized influence. Furthermore, for successful operation a man must be a hardworking gardener, a wage-earner, a cash cropper or a combination of these. Other qualities which are highly valued today as in the past are an even temper, wisdom in crises, intelligence, imagination and skill in oratory. Knowledge of sorcery and magic also contribute to prestige. Non-traditional activities can build up a man's reputation too. People with some education, and particularly those in skilled jobs, enjoy a high social status which does not depend entirely on their cash incomes. Teachers in village schools are deferred to socially by villagers to a very marked extent, as are other villagers home on leave from good jobs in towns. Partly because it enables a man to be generous and partly for its own sake, cash cropping on a large scale is also a source of prestige.

A distinction must be drawn however between high social status and political influence, although the former clearly contributes to the latter. I know of several comparatively highly educated and intelligent men who remain aloof from village politics as a result of personal inclination or incompetence in political manoeuvring. Several men renowned throughout the area for their 'generosity' have little or no influence in politics. I can think of two in particular in different villages who have a very high reputation as *lo man*. Neither has the talent nor the presence to be a dominant force. Some who are cash croppers on a fairly large scale, especially when they are young, deliberately cut themselves off economically, socially and politically from most of their neighbours so as to be able to build up their enterprises and re-invest their profits. One such man has planted 336 cocoa trees and 1,708 coconut palms. He lives on his plantation with his wife, children and elderly parents, at a considerable distance from the village, and appears to have no interest or influence in village politics. The foreign teacher working in Madang is another person with high status but no political influence. He is not a political substitute for the Madang man who is a teacher elsewhere, because it is rarely that a man's word is heard away from his home village or area. Another factor contributing to the isolation of foreign teachers is their high mobility between schools. Generally speaking, the political benefit which might be reaped in the village arena by those with a regular wage, comparatively good jobs, education and skills is rarely realized in Madang because such men, usually of necessity, live away from their home area.

A number of men, however, are politically influential in Madang without occupying, or at least in part independently of their occupancy of any formal position. It should be emphasized that they cannot be sharply distinguished from other Madangs, and that there are varying degrees of influence. There are many lesser or aspiring Big Men. For purposes of discussion I shall consider a limited number of such men, 21 in 16 villages. There are two each in Barahaim, Butelkud and Kamba, three in Korog and none in Yahil. The 21 were selected at the end of my fieldwork period by myself and my main informant, who is himself one of their number. My informant's two-fold definition of these men's role is a good starting point for the discussion. He said

[He] can be personally attacked but is still able to think about the welfare of the whole village. He can keep the peace and stop quarrels. He is a good helmsman (*em i holim sitia gut*) in the village. He makes peace after quarrels. He holds large feasts . . . A man is not a Big Man from one feast or one speech. It's a question of everything together.

In other words, from a position of some prestige in the community, a man carves out for himself a position of influence first by his specifically political abilities and secondly by his reputation for generosity and his network of credit. It is significant here that the 21 men under consideration were all mature, the youngest being 34 and their average age 50 years.

A man's first and most important sphere of influence is his own clan. The clan and its leading man or men support each other to their mutual advantage in the power struggles between clans and with other potential Big Men. Within the clan a Big Man may act as a father to others besides his own sons, taking the initiative in the marriage negotiations and brideprice payments of younger clansmen. All clansmen benefit from his good credit, prestige and influence in the wider community. His support is valuable in disputes, and they can call on him for loans. In return the Big Man has behind him a block of loyal supporters. They will vote for him, support his recommendations in the *tamaniak* and provide him with a docile and quickly mobilized work force. A good example of this relationship between clan and Big Man is given by my own dealings with the man who was mainly responsible for me in Kauris village. When I first arrived the villagers were unsure and suspicious of me. But my host was a Big Man, and his clansmen were organized to meet me and carry my baggage to their hamlet. Later on, when a new house was to be built for me, it was again my host's clansmen who did the work. For him there were several advantages in this arrangement. He could easily control and rely on the work force involved in the house building; the work appeared as merely an extension of the many services he rendered me, and his clansmen were grateful to him for the access he afforded them to cash payments. But all clansmen do not support a Big Man among their number all of the time. There are some issues, such as support for Yali, on which my host in Kauris is not in agreement with all his clan. In many other contexts they are, however, a valuable source of support.

The Big Man can also enjoy mutually advantageous relationships with non-agnatic cognates and affines, particularly in villages other than his own. Among the Big Men under consideration, 13 out of the 18 who are currently married (including one with two wives) have taken women from villages other

than their own, and one of the remaining five has chosen to stress
the ties between his wife and her natal family in another village,
as well as those with her adopting family in his own. His wife's
true brother is a Big Man himself in this other village. The
geographical extent of this type of extra-village support can be
deduced from the material on marriages in Chapter 3. Since
about 66 per cent of extra-village marriages within the District
are between villages less than three miles apart, the majority of
a man's extra-village affines and closest non-agnatic kinsmen
(e.g. MoBro, FaSis) will also be found within that distance.
Thus the extent of a Big Man's influence is restricted not only by
the practical limitations of recruitment to a personalized faction
but also by the actual location of members in it.

In practice, because of the solidarity of the village in terms of
residence, interests, marriage, history and social life and the
existence of the *tamaniak*, a Big Man can usually count as direct
supporters many of his fellow villagers as well as his clansmen.
In addition a Big Man can command support by virtue of non-
traditional patron-client ties, such as those between a man and
settlers on his land, or between an employer and his workmen.

My main divergence from the regular anthropological model
(e.g. Sahlins 1966) has been to describe traditional Madang Big
Men as optional operators in a political system of which important
structural features were decision by consensus and a plurality of
officials. Nor is the Big Man today the king-pin of intra-village
politics. The *tamaniak* is the framework within which he operates.
A Big Man may also be influential in the activities of other
organizations – the church, for example, or the cocoa cooperative.
But always he works within an institution in which decisions
can perfectly well be taken without him. Some Big Men are
more influential informally or in the *tamaniak* itself than others,
and a man's political purchase may vary from one occasion or
issue to another, particularly if he has a competitor within his
own village.

Sahlins (1966, pp. 165–6) makes a useful distinction between
the nature of a Big Man's relationship with his own committed
supporters and of that with the rest of his social universe. To his
own supporters a man is something of a leader, to the rest he is
just a 'man of renown', a famous but not necessarily politically
influential figure. In Madang it appears that the balance between

these two spheres varies from one individual to another. Some men appear to be influential within their own clan and village and among other kinsmen and affines, while not being particularly well-known elsewhere. Others are famous abroad as well as influential at home. These differences arise largely from the conjunction or otherwise of formal and informal leadership roles, a topic to which I now turn.

THE RELATIONSHIP BETWEEN FORMAL AND INFORMAL LEADERSHIP

Although I have so far isolated these two types of leadership for purposes of presentation, in practice a considerable number of men operate in both spheres and/or move from one to the other. Whether or not men *do* operate in both spheres is often crucial to their performance and achievement in either type of role. But one cannot say categorically either that the majority of officials are also Big Men or that the majority of Big Men are also officials. The evidence suggests that in both cases there is a fairly even division between the two alternatives. About half (19) of the 37 councillors were described by a panel of informants as Big Men, and of the 14 councillors who are currently occupying other positions, 8 are also Big Men. From Table 20 it appears that slightly under half of the 21 Big Men in the Madang villages are currently also officials, although more have occupied such positions in the past. Of course not all of these figures indicate which type of leadership was attained first, only that there is some overlap between them.

There are a number of possible reasons why the roles of official and Big Man should not coincide. The qualities expected of leaders in the two spheres are not necessarily combined in one individual. Voters in a council election may prefer a man with more skill in manipulating modern institutions to one who is a Big Man by virtue of traditionally prized abilities. In addition a number of the official positions discussed in this book cover several different villages, while Big Men are primarily important within only one. There are more Big Men in Madang than there are available positions of certain types. There are 21 Big Men in the 17 villages but only four councillors. However it does appear from Table 20 that the position of *komiti* is not normally held by a Big Man, although there is such a post in every village. Big

Men may choose not to occupy official positions. They may tire of the duties of office or, confident of their influence within their village, feel that they have little to gain by accepting additional onerous responsibilities. Several people expressed the opinion that younger and more educated men could do official work and leave their seniors to 'look after the village'.

Where Big Men do not hold official positions, power is likely to be dispersed within the village. In such cases the officials are

Table 20. Offices currently or previously occupied by 21 Big Men

Office	No. of men (total)	No. currently holding office
Councillor	7	3
Luluai	4	—
Lutheran school teacher	3	—
Komiti	2	2
Lo bos	2	2
Cooperative or R.P.S. official	2	—
Tultul	1	—
Lutheran pastor	1	1
Roman Catholic 'worker'	1	1
Member of circuit council	1	1
Land Titles Commissioner	1	1
Total no. of men	17	9

Notes: 1. Since not all 21 Big Men were interviewed, this table may under-estimate the number of previous positions held.
2. Of the four Big Men who have never held an office, it is interesting to note that three are the sons of luluai.

not as influential as they are elsewhere, and can in fact be in a very weak position if they fall foul of the Big Men. This has been the situation in some villages for a number of years. Thus in 1959/60 an Administration officer wrote that village (local government) officials were often 'front men' and had little real influence at home (D.D.A., Patrol Report No. 11 of 59/60, Madang District). But Big Men who do not reinforce their informal influence with official authority do not today enjoy so much extra-village renown as their counterparts who do.

Big Men who are also officials do not necessarily possess qualities which are likely to make them successful in both fields.

Although five of the six councillors who are most dominant in the council chamber are also Big Men in their home villages, four of the seven who say nothing in meetings are also Big Men at home. But wherever official and Big Man do coincide, there can be little doubt that the two roles reinforce each other. A councillor can use his standing and influence to rally support in elections and ward affairs. I have already cited several ways in which a man's affines and kinsmen can help him to be an effective councillor. The more influence a man has the more significant will this support be. Foreign clients can also be important. In the 1969 election, one aspiring Big Man mustered members of a settlement on his land, about one-quarter of those voting in the ward, in an unsuccessful attempt to replace another Big Man with his own nominee. Occupation of an office can also increase a man's influence among his supporters because he is in a position to distribute favours (among them: work, tax exemptions, information on sources of finance etc.). Even after he has ceased to be councillor, as a Big Man he may be able to draw on social credit built up during his period of tenure.

A distinction needs to be drawn between offices with a limited geographical and social range and those with a wider one. The position of Big Man can only reinforce relatively local-level offices such as councillor, *komiti* and *lo bos*, and can have little influence on success in roles such as council President or M.H.A. While many voters expect councillors to behave like Big Men, they look for something else from their representative in the House of Assembly. Candidates for the two positions muster support in different ways. The M.H.A. has to look beyond his own and nearby villages to voters most of whom he has never met. Peter Lawrence (1970, p. 97) describes this process for Angmai Bilas and John Poe (Yali's main opponent in 1968 in the Rai Coast Open): 'The distinctive feature of Angmai's and Poe's campaigns was their capacity to evaluate and exploit potential voting trends . . . They wooed the support of local government councillors, especially in distant parts of their electorates, and through them tried to keep in touch with the villagers.' In this kind of campaign being a Big Man (which neither of them were) would have been little help. In fact Bato Bultin, who is a Big Man at the local level, lost to Angmai Bilas who is not. It may be argued that Yali has very widespread support although his role is very similar to that of a traditional Big Man. But although Yali *acts* like a Big Man, he initially recruited his supporters not through inter-personal ties but through his activities on behalf of the Australian Administration. Although the role of Big Man may not assist multi-village officials in their careers and duties, their formal position may considerably enhance their status and influence at the local level.

When the Big Man is also an official, it is important to ask *which* particular position he holds. In a largely Christian village such as Nobanob, where the Big Man is also the pastor, the church organization is relatively more important than it is for example in Kauris where only about half the villagers are Christian and the councillor is the Big Man. It is doubtful whether the Big Man in Kauris would have been anywhere near so successful, given the allegiances of his village, if he had linked his political career with the church.

In addition to pluralism and movement between leadership roles, there is also unofficial personal interaction between leaders, as when fellow councillors attended the funeral of one of their President's children. On patrols councillors are usually entertained by and stay with the most prominent individuals in the villages they visit. In one village such patrols are regularly entertained by the Big Man in his guest house, not by the *komiti*, although the latter may help with food. Ties of kinship and affinity also exist between different leaders, although these are perhaps most common among the *lo bos* who are least geographically dispersed. There are other cases where contacts in public life have led to the development of personal friendships. The daughter of one Big Man is married to the President of the cooperative, who comes from a village a considerable distance from her home. Such a match was made both more likely and more acceptable by the prominence of the families involved. Friendships and contacts made in one sphere of leadership can be carried over to another. Church leaders turned councillors keep in touch with the people with whom they were working before.

8

Pragmatic and Ideological Conflict

In this chapter I approach the subject of inter-village integration through an analysis of political conflict in the sense of an opposition of interests. For convenience of presentation I have given names to the two types of conflict I describe for Madang. The terms 'pragmatic' and 'ideological' conflict are illustrated in Figure 2. Pragmatic conflict is that which arises in the first instance between villages and thereafter between combinations of villages. Ideological conflict in contrast cuts across village boundaries. While there is pragmatic conflict *within* each of the structures described in Chapter 7, ideological conflict is outside any single one of them and is concerned with relationships *between* structures.

PRAGMATIC CONFLICT

In Madang pragmatic conflicts arise between coordinate units within administrative structures. Such coordinate units appear at different levels and their number and range vary from one structure to another. Figure 2 indicates only three of these levels – village and then first and second levels of combination – whereas in local government there are more coordinate units – village, ward, council, district and nation. As suggested in Part II, the amount of conflict within different structures varies. Differences between council and church, for example, are related to the extent to which these institutions are mainly concerned with collecting and distributing resources which appear to the actors to be scarce.

When pragmatic conflict exists between village-level units, it does not matter whether everyone in the villages concerned is a member of such a unit or not. Since the conflict arises *within* an administrative structure, what is important is the political relationship between, for example, the Christian community in one village and that in the next. The relationship between Christians and non-Christians in their own village is irrelevant. Generally speaking, pragmatic conflicts arise between rather than within villages, but coordinate units do appear within the village in inter-clan rivalry, either for land or for more generalized power. Case 7 shows how such competition may focus on leading men in different clans.

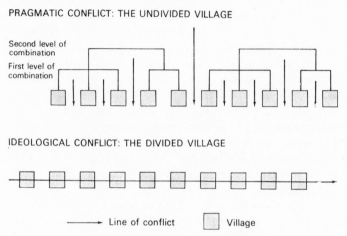

PRAGMATIC CONFLICT: THE UNDIVIDED VILLAGE

Second level of combination

First level of combination

IDEOLOGICAL CONFLICT: THE DIVIDED VILLAGE

Line of conflict ☐ Village

Fig. 2. The two types of conflict

Case 7. Two rival clans

B. and K. are two clans in a single village. G. of K. clan was paramount *luluai* in the period immediately before the Second World War. Another prominent and ambitious man in the village was T. in B. clan. Both men had considerable support from their clans. T.'s ambition was to become *luluai*, so he started a campaign to oust G. K. was acting at this time as G.'s assistant. With evidence supplied by fellow clansmen, T. managed to get G. jailed for abuse of his powers as a government official. In particular he was accused of inflicting illegal physical penalties. By this manoeuvre T. succeeded G. as the most prominent man in the village in government eyes, although he did not actually capture the paramountcy, which was suspended. But the matter did not rest there. K. clan were bitter about their leader's defeat. For many years they employed magical means to try to bring down T., and even today – a long time after G.'s death – they give him negligible support in his role as their councillor.

While the village remains largely undisturbed by pragmatic conflict, it also appears to be the most active unit in it. Thus I have argued that in Madang the village is more significant in terms of perceptions, interests and conflict than the ward, area or whole council. This is due in part to the number of different administrative functions which cluster at village level and at least in some cases reinforce one another. But, particularly when one remembers the different degrees of participation in the various organizations which take the village as their base unit, other factors contributing to the importance of the village must be examined. The village is a group of land-owning clans, and most of its members live relatively near to one another. It follows then that many interests (for instance in roads and schools) will focus on this, the local unit. There is also a concentration of kinship and affinal ties within the village, and feasts and dances are commonly held at that level. Furthermore the *tamaniak* facilitates the mobilization of opinion and the discussion of disputes within the village. No land-based interests or social ties unite the persons comprehended at the supra-village levels of formal structures.

The village also seems to be important in people's perception of their political environment. Legends and traditions encourage a sense of village identity. Of the four original 'Wagi' villages which survive today, Kamba is the proud and acknowledged original land-owner and ancestral founder (*het bilong graun na het bilong sitori*). Kamba informants became very anxious when they thought I was confused on this point. Villages are also believed to have inherited characteristics which determine their history. The story goes that in ancestral times a Kauris man was quick to reply to an enquirer from the coast that his land was occupied. Silabob's ancestor, although he was nearer, hung back and did not respond. So today people say Kauris has stolen a march on Silabob in commercial development because its destiny is to go first and Silabob's to follow slowly behind. The village is a familiar concept, whereas the House of Assembly electorate and the upper levels of the local government hierarchy are not. It also epitomizes for many, especially older men, a good if vanished way of life. They hanker for village consensus and disapprove of majority voting. One old man told me, 'The Christian way of life has lost its grip (*i go malomalo*). The village way of life too has fallen down.' In the old days, it is said, men were taller, boys obedient and sexual relations before marriage rare. Although there is certainly a romantic element in old men's accounts of the past, such comments reflect a more widespread malaise. Many people perceive a lack of harmony and order – witness the emphasis in many cargo cults on a need for improvement in just these areas.

IDEOLOGICAL CONFLICT

Although ideological conflict may be expressed in other ways, I shall discuss here only one major form which immediately strikes the observer and is mentioned by informants over and over again. This is, broadly speaking, a two-sided conflict, and is perceived as such by the actors themselves. It is commonly said that 'We Madangs are divided into two camps (*mipela Madang i bruk tupela lain*)'. The focus of this extremely acrimonious conflict in Madang is one man living some 50 miles away from the area, namely Yali. His opponents fall into two categories: all Christians are unambiguously anti-Yali and a number of non-Christians are also avowedly opposed to him. In terms of formal structure there is a contrast between the two sides. While Yali's supporters are all members of his movement and are thus comparatively well organized, his opponents do not fit neatly into one institutional framework. The church gives to and receives considerable support from other institutions in its conflict with Yali. I find it helpful to see the opposition to Yali as being a sort of alliance between several different organizations. Some of the administrative structures considered in this book (namely the Workers' Association, the Land Titles Commission, the Parents and Citizens' Associations, and the *tamaniak*) are irrelevant to the conflict between Yali and his opponents. Others, particularly the church and the council, are involved in it. Opposition to Yali seems to come simultaneously from several directions because of the diffuseness of his aims and interests. Since his movement has religious, social, political and economic aspirations, it encounters hostility on a number of fronts which in a western social structure would be institutionally differentiated.

The first focus for opposition which I shall discuss is the church, in the area under study particularly the Lutheran church. To be a supporter of Yali and a church member are mutually exclusive.

L

Opposition from the mission was first directed against Yali's polygyny and his retinue of unmarried women, and was hardened by his reversion to paganism. It is still bitter today. The indigenous Lutheran church workers are particularly outspoken in their hostility in sermons, warnings and advice to fellow Christians. One preacher I heard said from the pulpit, 'Yali is a false prophet, a wolf in sheep's clothing'. The general tenor of Yali's relations with the church is illustrated by the rumour that when his 'day of independence' dawned on 1 August 1969, all Christians would have their throats cut. That Christians too dream of getting the upper hand is illustrated by another rumour that I heard at the 1968 Amele Circuit conference. It was whispered that Yali's tongue had got shorter so that he could not speak much. He had asked a Lutheran headman to pray for him and had then recovered. For his part Yali attacks the church for having tricked the people into giving up the pagan ritual which sustained their forefathers and is their only hope for the future. As one informant put it, 'The mission and white men have stolen these things. We've followed the Bible and some people have died without any improvement [in material conditions].' Another man summed up the present position, 'A follower of Yali does not go to church. Yali himself does not go . . . Now feeble men can go if they want to.' Those who were previously given a Christian baptism have it 'washed away' with Yali's new baptism.

Ambenob Council is another focus for opposition to Yali. In the council chamber apathy in the wards, neglect of roads and cocoa blocks and failure to vote and pay taxes are often attributed, not always fairly, to Yali. The council's attitudes are best illustrated by its attempts (entirely *ultra vires*) to ban Yali's emissary from the council area. When Yali's right hand man, Dui, visited Madang in March 1969 he and two *lo bos* were summoned before the Executive and Finance Committee. Dui was told that he should have reported to the President before he travelled inland, and that he must not come to Ambenob area again except in his official capacity as a member of the Rai Coast Local Government Council. In July the same committee followed this up with a letter to the District Commissioner, saying that the council did not want Dui to come to Ambenob area again (A.L.G.C., Minute 3-4, Executive and Finance Committee Meeting, 29 July 1969). The council's attitude to Yali is known and resented among his supporters. A man from Kauris is said to have been reprimanded by the District Commissioner for sending $10 to Yali and the Administration has at times come out clearly against financial contributions to Yali on the grounds that people are wasting their hard-won dollars. One informant commented that 'the council would have liked to send us all to prison, but the D.C. said no'.

It is worth while considering why Ambenob Council is so vehemently anti-Yali. Clearly its close ties with the Administration and its own roots in Western culture give it little common ground with the cultists. This position is reinforced by the affiliation of individual councillors. Only three out of the 37 are pro-Yali, although in the villages under study, for example, 34 per cent of those resident in the Sub-District support him. Not only are the Yali councillors in the minority, but they are also among the least active participants in council affairs. Table 21 shows that none of the three holds any council office, and that 34 out of 35 positions are held by Christians. All three pro-Yali councillors are among the seven members who are not recorded in the minutes as taking any part at all in council meetings. This is probably related to the fact that they come from wards which were only included in the council in 1967, and therefore have little experience. Furthermore they have to travel long distances and frequently do not attend. Indeed one was formally removed from the council for this reason (A.L.G.C., Minute 15-4, General Meeting, 9 January 1969).

The Administration is another, if less important, focus for opposition to Yali. Although its official policy is neutrality, there is some deviation even at the highest level in the District. At a Tax Payers' Meeting in Amele on 20 January 1969, the District Commissioner said, 'If you have cargo cultists left, throw them out, shut their mouths'. This attitude of the D.C. and his staff is well known to the people. One supporter of Yali saw it reflected in Administration handling of charges against the Regional candidate who teamed with Yali in the 1968 elections.

When Whitaker was in the police [he was in fact in the Corrective Institutions Branch] he helped Yali to become famous (*gerapim nem*). He was thrown out of the police force because he supported Yali . . .

He is not a New Guinean. So the Government asked him what he was doing helping them and living with them.

A final and even less well-defined focus for hostility to Yali is the general principle of modern western economic development as

Table 21. Affiliation of councillors who hold other offices on the council

Office	Roman Catholic	Lutheran	Total Christian	Neither	Yali	All
Committee members:						
Agriculture	1	5	6	—	—	6
Executive and Finance	1	7	8	1	—	9
Health	4	3	7	—	—	7
Market Trustees	1	3	4	—	—	4
Tax Review (8/68)	—	6	6	—	—	6
Portfolio members:						
Agriculture	1	—	1	—	—	1
Education	—	1	1	—	—	1
Public Works	—	1	1	—	—	1
Total number of offices	8	26	34	1	0	35
Percentage of all offices	22·8	74·3	97·1	2·9	0	100
No. of councillors	7	23	30	4	3	37
Percentage of total	18·9	62·2	81·1	10·7	8·1	100

Note: The president is a member of the Executive and Finance Committee, a Lutheran and *ex officio* the Portfolio Member for District Administration.

embodied in the rural progress societies and later the cooperatives. For example, I have already mentioned that the issue in the national elections was economic development, and the choice was between Yali's 'road' on the one hand and western economic progress on the other.

These different elements in the opposition to Yali – the church, the council, the Administration and modern economic institutions – reinforce one another. The Administration obviously supports with funds and/or personnel the council and cooperatives which it helped to establish, but the other relationships I describe are less obvious and may be more peculiar to the Madang scene. Separately the council and mission oppose Yali, but simultaneously they strengthen each other's position. A councillor will sometimes where politic add Christian arguments to his own secular discussion of council affairs. Churchmen urge their flocks to be good citizens, pay their taxes and support the council. Council matters may be raised informally at church meetings. At one circuit conference an assistant pastor mentioned to another delegate (who happened to be the council President) that there had been trouble on the plantation where he worked. The matter was raised for attention by the council. There is also formal recognition of the tie between church and council. All Ambenob meetings open with prayers. But perhaps most significant of all, the council grants automatic tax reductions (A.L.G.C., Minute 15-3, General Meeting, 4 June 1969) to certain classes of church worker (a privilege not even extended to its own council *komiti*). The explanation of this close tie can be found in the material already presented on personnel in church and council. Of the 37 councillors 30 are Christians and many of these currently hold or have previously held office in their respective churches. The alliance between church and council is apparent to Yali's supporters. One explained to me why Yali's promises had not been fulfilled: 'If the mission and council hadn't pulled him down (*daunim em*) it would have happened'.

The church also supports Western forms of economic development in both word and deed. It preaches that money cannot be acquired without an effort. Only by hard work and with God's help can a man improve his financial position. One evangelist told me that, 'It is not possible to get money from prayers. The Bible says we can only get it from commercial enterprises (*bisnis*), from working with our hands. The Holy Spirit will help us.' Many Christians as well as pagans are not sure that there may not be effective money-making magic. But most of them think that such magic is either less profitable than cash cropping or, even if it is successful, is wicked. The church also lends practical encouragement to the activities it advocates. In the initial stages of the Foran Rural Progress Society it provided $300 to buy a rice milling machine. When the society was wound up, the machine was given to the young people's group of the Lutheran church which was already engaged in rice and coffee cultivation on its own behalf.

And the council advocates cash cropping. The relation between economic and political development was recognized by the local M.H.A. (also a councillor) at one Tax Payers' Meeting, when he said, 'The only thing you can do is commercial enterprise. In the future your taxes will have to build your country, so you must earn money now and get things going.' Frequently councillors urge their people to persevere with cash cropping. The council was the original agency which handled the processing and marketing of cocoa beans produced in its own Ambenob Cocoa Project. It was not until 1964 that the council handed over these duties and the associated plant to the Kumul Cocoa Project, as it was then called (D.A.S.F., File 23-3-1(2)).

There is also less specific hostility. In general his opponents grumble about the sexual side of Yali's rituals and other suspected nefarious practices. In the field I was confronted with the words of my own academic discipline on the lips of my informants. The phrase *kago kal* (cargo cults) is well-known in Madang. It is used as a term of disapprobation with reference to Yali. It implies something so widely disapproved (and equally widely ill-defined) that even Yali's supporters wish to dissociate themselves from it. Similarly, Yali's movement blames its difficulties on its opponents in general. One supporter said, 'If we had all followed Yali's work together, his new way of life would have arrived long ago'.

I turn now to consider the particular forms taken by the ideological conflict between supporters and opponents of Yali. Within villages they vary. Often Christians oppose cultists (as in Kauris); sometimes cultists are opposed by other non-Christians (as in Mirkuk); and sometimes Christians combine with non-Christians against Yali's supporters (as in Korog). In some villages there is no division at all, because everyone is on one side or the other (as in Yahil and Mis). In those villages where there are two distinct factions, social relations between the two sides are often restricted. For example, one Yali man said of the anti-Yali councillor in his village, 'I don't go to K.'s house. If we sit down with the other lot they would only make trouble for us.' The hostility is very personalized within the village. One man said, 'Yali is what I like. I don't mind if people report me to police, Administration etc. I'll go to court. L., D., I. and K. [prominent members of the anti-Yali faction in his village] are no good. They say Yali is no good.' The existence of such a division in a village may give rise to direct if somewhat *ad hoc* conflict. Its very existence reduces the means of resolving personal disputes. Followers of Yali have recourse to the *lo bos* and the Yali moral code, but in dealings between adherents of different sides these are irrelevant. The disputes that reflect the division most closely are those arising directly from the attitudes of the two sides. On one occasion a Yali faction refused the rest of the village access to a building owned by Ambenob Council which it was proposed should be used for a council-sponsored women's club. The building stood on the land of a Yali supporter, but the women in the club were all Christians. When they came to cut the grass around the hut, the landowner drove them away. In another case a youth was bitten by a snake. His parents believed that his death might in some way hasten the arrival of Yali's cargo, and so did not take him to the nearby medical aid post. His death led to great bitterness between his Christian and cultist relatives. In other cases the division has exacerbated pre-existing quarrels. For instance in Case 1 (A coconut planter operating on another clan's land) hostility appears to have been the more intense because one brother is a Lutheran headman and the other a supporter of Yali. The Yali faction as a whole in the village concerned seems to be trying to make capital out of this dispute.

Writing of cargo cults among the Toaripi of Papua, Dawn Ryan (1969, p. 110) has said that 'it is not the message but the call to action which sparks opposition'. In Madang too it is not the dogma of the cultists but their actions or in many cases their inaction which create so much hostility. The *lo bos* and cultists represent a challenge to the councillor and church worker. Cultists prefer to solve their disputes and heal their ailments without reference to the Western institutions with which the councillor identifies. By not taking their problems to him they reduce his standing at home, with Administration officials and with the council at large. Typically cultists give less support than Christians to the councillor's meetings or projects. At a village meeting in October 1968, 8 of a possible 15 Christians were present, but only 3 of 16 cultists. It may be that cultists pay their taxes less readily than others, but my figures are not very conclusive. In August 1968 in Kauris, 11 of 13 Yali supporters liable for tax, but only 7 of 11 Christians, had defaulted for that financial year. The Kamba tax courts discussed in Chapter 6 illustrate the same tendency. In a different sphere the Lutheran headman also finds himself competing with the *lo bos* for followers.

Conflict beyond the village is largely associated with particular multi-village institutions. The reaction of council and church to Yali has already been discussed. Cargo was also a perceived issue in the 1968 House of Assembly elections. Through the network of kinship and affinal ties there is considerable contact between members of the two sides, and the division between cultists and opponents may occasionally exacerbate or give rise to disputes in this field too. Even villages within which there is no division on the Yali issue are involved in the inter-village arena of conflict between the two sides. The people of Mis, for instance, are loud in their condemnation of Yali, and are particularly vocal on the subject in relation to the church.

The position of the cultists in this conflict is somewhat paradoxical. In Gluckman's terms (1956, p. 46) they are on the one hand proposing rebellion and on the other seeking revolution. The paradox arises from the multiplicity, diffuseness and sometimes inconsistency of the aims and interests of Yali's cult. In the national elections those who voted for Yali were seeking a change of personnel within a given system. In their search for European-type wealth they are looking for a redistribution of resources rather than rejecting the value of such resources.[1] In many other respects, however, Yali's followers are aiming at larger changes in the system itself and at a completely different way of life. They reject such European institutions as Christianity, courts, Western medicine and (in part) the council and national House of Assembly, preferring traditional methods and forms of organization, or alternatively the recognition of Yali as 'king'. Yali's revolution involves a return to the past, but in Gluckman's terms the word is apt.

[1] For a parallel argument see Douglas 1970, p. 139.

In this context there is no common arena for the conflict, no equality of position in a single institutional framework. There are not two political parties confronting each other in a legislature, or two competing enterprises. To use Bailey's vocabulary (1969, pp. 15–16), we are dealing not with two sides playing the same game but with rival political structures, 'the criterion being the absence of an agreed set of rules which could regulate their conflict' (1969, p. 16). Thus one side cannot be called the establishment and the other the opposition, nor is one side in and the other out of power, because the two groups are not seeking power in the same terms. This (in addition to inadequacies of fieldwork) may help to explain the somewhat unsatisfactory nature of my description of conflict between the two sides. Despite the enormous difference between them, there is very little direct confrontation.[1]

I am far from suggesting that this type of opposition is found wherever there are cargo cults. But I think this analysis brings out the significance of relations between the cult, in itself a political structure, and what Bailey (1969, Chapter 1) has called its 'environment'. In some areas cargo cults may be found within other political structures, and the conflict between supporters and opponents may be institutionally regulated in more contexts than it is in Madang. In the Astrolabe Bay Local Government Council, which borders on Ambenob to the south, the President is an eminent supporter of Yali, the Vice-president an equally eminent anti-Yali man, and the councillors are divided between the two sides (P. L. McLaren, personal communication, 1970). Yali himself is a member of his home council on the Rai Coast, although the majority of his fellow councillors do not support him. Again Schwartz (1962, p. 383) describes the second cult on Manus as a division within the wider Paliau movement.

Analysis in terms of Bailey's model of political structures is also helpful in comparing the nationalist potential of the two sides, especially Yali's movement on the one hand and its overtly political counterpart, Ambenob Council, on the other. Yali's movement has much of the spirit of nationalism as it has appeared elsewhere, while the council is fairly conservative. On the whole

---

[1] Susan Robertson and I have discussed the effect on explanations of the Madang earthquake of the absence of even hostile contact (Hogg and Robertson 1971, p. 310).

Yali's opponents sympathize with the council and greatly fear self-government and independence. This situation underlines a second if related paradox – that of nationalism in rural areas. While a nationalist movement often harks back to traditional values and culture, its aim is defined largely in terms of the political and economic institutions of the colonial authority it wishes to overthrow. Turning once again to Bailey's terminology we could say that in its nationalist aspirations Yali's movement wants to play the game (in the world polity and economy) and at the same time to change the rules (remould these institutions in traditional terms). In fact, it is its traditionalism that militates against the fulfilment of its other aspirations, and makes it impossible for the cult to constitute an effective political organization. The anti-Yali political group for its part is aware of the rules of the nationalist game, and already operates within the general framework of the modern polity. Accordingly it is better qualified to be effective as a nationalist movement, but, as we have seen, it is not motivated in this direction. So nationalist activity in Madang is a case of those who would do cannot and those who could will not.

OPERATIONAL RELATIONSHIP BETWEEN PRAGMATIC AND IDEOLOGICAL CONFLICT

Logically, pragmatic and ideological conflict are incompatible. In the former a man makes common cause with all members of his own village in opposition to outsiders. In the latter he makes common cause with what is usually a section within his own village and with like-minded sections outside. Madangs today are faced with alternative foci for political identification, foci which can be grouped broadly into two kinds corresponding with the two types of conflict. The choice which they make varies according to the context and the issue. Of course this is also true *within* the framework of pragmatic conflict. A man can perceive his interests in terms of his village, ward or council according to the resources for which he is competing. In the national elections, or in discussions on the value of cash cropping, ideological rather than pragmatic conflict is significant. But on other occasions village identity is more important than the disagreement between Yali's supporters and opponents. At Tax Payers' Meetings, in council elections, in competitive inter-village dances and in arguments about transport on market days, the village comes first and ideological differences are forgotten.

On still other occasions, while there is actually no conflict with outsiders, village unity may be stressed and/or the line between cultists and others ignored. Thus the division is irrelevant in many marriage and land disputes, as is illustrated by Case 8.

Case 8. A runaway wife

S., a follower of Yali, was married to L., a Christian from his own village. L. was a dominant character and much stronger and more ambitious than her husband. She became friendly with the driver of the truck which collected people from her village to go to market and ran away to town to live with him. A meeting of the village *tamaniak* was held at which both S. and L. were present. From the Yali faction eight men and two women attended. Nine Christian men and four women were also present plus three people who were aligned with neither side.

The main speakers at the meeting were four cultists and seven Christians. All blamed the woman whose character, they said, was such that she was incapable of being faithful to one man. No Christian defended her. All combined to criticise her in no uncertain terms. The girls who had acted as go-betweens in her correspondence with her lover were also reprimanded. Since L. was suspected of adultery with S.'s father it was agreed that the case could not be taken to court. Throughout there was appeal to generally accepted rules of conduct for the marriage relationship and agreement that L. had contravened these. There was no partisanship in terms of the cargo issue. In fact the only criticism of the husband came from a fellow supporter of Yali who said:

> I warned you when you got engaged. You will put on her dress and she will put on your trousers. That is the kind of woman she is.

It was agreed that S. and L. should be divorced. There were no children and no brideprice had been paid.

There are other questions on which both ideological and pragmatic conflict seem at least partly irrelevant, and on which the majority of Madangs appear to agree. The Ambenob Council is unpopular with many who are not cultists, and some attitudes towards Europeans are widely shared. As a Lutheran headman complained, 'Europeans don't come and sit down with us and teach us how to live'. There is also much disillusionment about the failure to reward war and government service. But I think it would be true to say that in discussion of most of these issues the cultists are likely to be the more outspoken.

As a final example of the contextual nature of the two types of conflict, I shall discuss the role of the Christian councillor in a partly cargo ward and show how this position can be involved in both types of conflict on different occasions. Wards 2, 3 and 4, which cover 12 of the villages under study, contain respectively 43 per cent, 49 per cent and 39 per cent cultists. It seems to me unlikely that villagers, especially in Ward 3, would be aware of the exact voting strength of each side and in fact informants generally felt that these wards were fairly evenly divided. In the 1967 and 1969 elections, however, only 2 of the 11 Madang candidates in these wards were supporters of Yali, and neither was successful. In view of the strength of his movement in the area this is surprising, particularly for Ward 2 in 1969, where the opposition to cargo cult was split between three other candidates. A possible explanation, and one that certainly applies to Kamba in 1969, is that cultists are so hostile to the council that they do not bother to vote. But a second explanation has more widespread significance. In elections voters are concerned with the interests of their village or ward vis-à-vis other villages and wards, in other words with pragmatic conflict. All members of a village or ward, be they cultists or non-cultists, are equally implicated in tax rates, village labour and council benefits so they are out to find the best men to represent them. They may do this either by voting for their own village candidate in preference to one from another village or by electing the best man in the whole ward. One cultist (who is typical of many) explained why he voted Christian: 'K. does a good job. S. [the cargo candidate from another village] doesn't know a lot about government work.' In the national elections, in contrast, ideological conflict is decisive for cultists. But when we look at the way the Christian councillor operates within his ward once he has been elected, we find that ideological conflict once again becomes important; he competes with the *lo bos* and receives less cooperation from the cultists than the Christians.

A COMPARISON BETWEEN THE TWO TYPES OF CONFLICT IN TERMS OF INTEGRATION

I do not use the word 'integration' in any mystical sense. I refer specifically to the situation in which an individual identifies with others beyond his own village, perceives common interests with them and acts in terms of these interests. There is a contrast here between pragmatic and ideological conflict; the latter has given rise to a much greater degree of integration. The difference is due in part to the relationship of each to the village. Pragmatic conflict has reinforced the village's pre-existing tendency towards autonomy and the paramountcy of village interests. Ideological conflict has created a sense of identity beyond the village just because it has divided the village internally. It follows in part what are largely forms of economic differentiation within the village. Such an analysis may have wider implications. While pragmatic conflict in segmentary structures is not likely to diminish regionalism of various kinds, organizations that can divide regions, and even smaller groups such as villages, may be more effective in creating some identity of interest at the national level.

But in Madang there are other reasons why ideological conflict has led to greater integration between villages. These derive from the particular character of Yali's movement and the kind of opposition that it generates. In these respects his movement can be contrasted with Ambenob Council. As I have already indicated, within the council there is keen competition for scarce resources. There is no such competition among Yali's followers, since the resources with which they are concerned are both ill-defined and conceptually unlimited. Similarly Yali's opponents, as far as their opposition to him is concerned, are not divided by internal conflicts. They are concerned with general principles. A further feature of ideological conflict in Madang is the acrimony it creates, and the intensity of commitment to one side or the other. Race relations, the place of tradition, the decline in morality and continuing monetary poverty in the villages, are all vitally important issues in Madang eyes. It is these that Madangs see as involved in the conflict over Yali. Attitudes towards him are expressed in words and actions of almost religious fervour. In contrast, people do not see their allegiance to Ambenob Council or to the whole nation as directly related to these burning questions. Ideological conflict in Madang centres on one person who has inspired great personal loyalty and admiration among his followers and bitter hatred among his enemies. The same kind of appeal or hostility cannot be said to attach to bodies of elected representatives, or to the occupants of non-traditional official positions.

A BACKWARD GLANCE AT THE METHOD

In this book I have attempted to produce an overall view of political life in 17 villages and to see, not just the parts, but the form of the whole. The choice of villages for inclusion was largely immaterial. A study of a different combination would very likely have produced similar results. But to have studied a number of villages rather than only one does seem to have been important. I made few assumptions about the significance of the village, and was under no compulsion to start with this entity as my key unit. The selection of area has also left me free to conclude that in a certain type of political conflict the village was less relevant than in another.

Through starting with a number of villages, I avoided preconceptions as to what was or was not political. I did not focus my study exclusively on Ambenob Council, but took as the basis for observation everything that happened in these villages, although of course I was able neither to observe nor to record anywhere near everything. It was thus that I was able to identify a type of political conflict that was not fought out within any formal institutional framework and, above all, was not one between factions within the council. It seems to me that this kind of approach is what the anthropologist has to offer in studies of developing nations. More and more specialists look at particular activities. Political scientists, economists and students of religion all have their own interests. But the anthropologist, if only at the grass-roots level, can observe relationships between local government councils, cooperatives, churches and cults, in other words, between the data usually observed by various specialists. Such an exercise would seem to me to have been valuable in Madang, if it has shown both the limits of the relevance of particular institutions and the kinds of political decisions that men, standing in some sense outside them, make in relation to them.

Postscript, 1972[1]

National political parties first attracted the attention and support
of Madang villagers in the year 1970. In this postscript I shall
consider who supported which party at the time of the 1972
national elections and the relationship of these parties to the two
types of conflict discussed in Chapter 8. I have already shown how
in 1968 and 1969 the views of cargo cultists and their opponents
were polarized on self-government and independence. By 1972
the opposition to self-government was not as strong as it had been,
and opinions were divided rather on the *timing* of self-government. Even conservatives accepted that it was inevitable, and
wished only to delay it until there was a larger number of skilled
Papua New Guineans and the country was better developed
economically and capable of defence against external aggressors.
Cargo cultists for their part saw self-government in a much more
favourable, if somewhat millenial, light. As one *lo bos* told me,
'I am still living in a grass hut. If self-government comes I shall
have a good house, good chairs and a happy heart.' Other
cultists said they favoured early self-government because it would
mean the end of quarrels and adultery, because political development to date had brought no harm and because New Guineans
should be able to run their own country. On the latter grounds I
also found a handful of Christians in favour of early self-
government.

By 1972 three political parties were active in the Madang Sub-
District – the Pangu, People's Progress and United parties, the
two most influential being United and Pangu. In the Open

[1] This section is based on four weeks' supplementary fieldwork in Madang
in 1972. I spent three weeks there in January and February up to seven days
before polling began, and a further week in May after the new members had
taken their seats in the House. During my visits I interviewed informants in all 17
villages, a total of 54 different men, and after the election was able to ask everyone
in Kauris which way they had voted. Professor and Mrs P. Lawrence and Mrs A.
Bolger were also studying aspects of the Madang Open electorate, and I am
grateful to all three for the opportunity to discuss events and interpretation.
For a more detailed account of this study see Morauta (in press b).

election[1] these parties endorsed three of the six candidates, and in the Regional two (or possibly all[2]) of the three men who stood. In the Regional election voting in the Madang villages was not clearly on party lines for a number of reasons. The dual electorate system was not understood; Regional candidates campaigned little; Shong's position was ambiguous; and some voters identified the United and People's Progress parties. I shall therefore confine my remarks to the Open election. In this Job Sogasog of Foran was the Pangu candidate, Angmai Bilas of Riwo, the sitting member, stood for United, and a townsman, Kaukesa Kamo, was endorsed by P.P.P. At the time of my study neither Pangu nor United, both of which claimed extensive village membership, had comprehensive lists for the villages under study. However, party *komiti* men had been appointed in several villages and were widely known as such. The first plank in Pangu's platform was 'Pangu wants self-government now' (Somare 1972, p. 48). Although the United Party did not give its views on self-government such prominence in its official policy (Abal 1972, p. 25), the outspoken Pangu position, at least in Madang, appeared to focus the attention of both United and P.P.P. very much on the same question. Thus the parties emphasized a debate which was already of considerable interest to Madangs.

Although in 1972 there were wide variations in understanding of what political parties were, Madangs were by no means as hostile to them as they had been in 1968 (see Harding and Lawrence 1971, p. 173). It was understood that party support gave weight to a member's voice in the House, although some informants still expressed doubts about their possible divisive effects. There was also uncertainty about the precise policies of different parties. It was generally agreed that Pangu was in favour of early self-government, but there was much debate as to whether whites would be thrown out of the country at that stage. While many United supporters said this was Pangu's aim, Pangu supporters themselves vigorously denied this. One explained to me that 'Whites can stay. Australians, missionaries and private enterprise

---

[1] In 1972 the old Mabuso Open was reduced in size and renamed the Madang Open.

[2] The position of the third, Shong Babob, was not clear. He was certainly claimed by the United Party in the *Papua New Guinea Post-Courier* (17 February, pp. 14–15), but he himself in at least some public meetings and also in private interview denied the association.

must work together to help our country.' Pangu also attracted
support because it was believed to emphasize traditional New
Guinean customs. One cultist who was perhaps a little confused
over the definition of a political party told me that 'If you want
to make a little party with Pangu you can put on only traditional
dress and dance. You must not wear modern clothes.' Others
favoured Pangu because they saw it as a progressive party,
while United was seen as seeking to maintain an undesirable
status quo. Opposition to Pangu focussed mainly on the self-
government issue, but was also aroused by its hostility to that
rather ill-defined body, 'the Government', its urban bias, its
'unrealistic wage policy' and its platform planks concerned with
land. United Party was closely identified with the sitting member,
who had brought the party to Madang, and was seen as a vigor-
ous opponent of Pangu and early self-government. The party,
and more immediately its candidate, were credited with much
of the recent development in Madang (e.g. a feeder road to
Kamba) but were sometimes criticized for a supposed alliance
with the interests of whites. Villagers were generally ignorant
of the policies of P.P.P., although (following the Regional
P.P.P. candidate) they supposed that these were closer to those
of United than Pangu.

In the villages under study the election was a straight fight
between Angmai and Job. Together they obtained 97 per cent
of valid votes in Box 31,[1] which was located at Barahaim and
later Kamba and contained votes from 13 of the 17 villages under
study. In the Open electorate as a whole Angmai won on the
third count from Job. Both Angmai and Job had campaigned
extensively in the 17 villages, and on the whole party supporters
voted according to their chosen party. Thus in Kauris 36 out of
41 voters voted according to their previously expressed party
affiliations. Of the remainder three made mistakes, one United
supporter voted for an independent candidate, and one Pangu
supporter deliberately spread his votes between all three major
parties so that in any event his vote would not be wasted. While
party affiliation was significant both negatively and positively
for the two major candidates, Angmai certainly also attracted

---

[1] Figures taken from Department of Social Development and Home Affairs,
Tally sheets used in counting votes in Madang Open electorate, 1972.

M

votes on his personal record as sitting member, while Job probably lost some through his reputation for hard drinking, shifting
from one job to another and untrustworthiness.

Although both Angmai and Job polled well in their home
areas, the distribution of votes between them cannot be explained
entirely or even mainly in these terms. In the Open electorate as
a whole both must have received the majority of their votes
from people with whom they had no traditional cultural or social
ties whatever. The same trend is clear in the 13 Madang villages
which cast their votes in Box 31. Here Angmai won, if narrowly,
in what can only be described as his main opponent's home area.
The main lines of party support in Madang followed not the
segmentary localized divisions defined by pragmatic conflict,
but the ideological division between cultists and their opponents,
a division which cut across villages and language groups. Broadly
speaking, the cultists voted Pangu and their opponents United.
For instance in Kauris, a village almost evenly divided between
the two sides, 16 men and 7 women were paid-up members of
United Party and all of these were Christians (from *komiti*'s
hand-written record, dated 6 December 1971). In Madang as a
whole 26 of my 33 Christian informants intended to vote for
Angmai, while only two of them declared a preference for Job
and Pangu. Of the 17 cargo cultists interviewed, 15 said they
would vote for Job, while the remaining two did not know.
Of the four men interviewed who neither supported Yali nor
went to church, three said they would vote for Pangu and one
for United. While these interviews do not constitute a random
sample, the same pattern emerges in Kauris, where I interviewed
everybody who voted. Twenty-five out of 36 Christians voted
for Angmai and three of the remainder said they voted for Job
but supported United Party. Seven of the eight cargo cultists
voted Pangu in the Open, and the two unaligned men voted for
Angmai.

There was not a 100 per cent fit between the cargo/anti-cargo
division on the one hand and the Pangu/United party division
on the other. A tiny minority of Christians supported Pangu
on policy grounds – particularly in Job's home village – and
there may also have been one or two personal votes for Job from
kinsmen and affines in Panim and Foran. In Barahaim a number
of men unaligned in the cargo/Christian conflict supported

Pangu in the election. Among cultists, one or two did not vote
Pangu because they were afraid that Job as a Christian would not
follow Yali's true road.

The alliance between Pangu and Yali's movement can be
attributed to a number of factors, although I would not argue for
the priority of any single one. In the first place, Angmai and Job
held contrasting attitudes to the pre-existing political divisions
in the area. While Angmai was unambiguously opposed to cargo
cult and in favour of Christianity, the council, the cooperative
and cash cropping, Job had developed a very different personal
philosophy. He believed that if a man was to be a true leader in
Madang he had to lead both sides, cargo cultists and Christians;
he had to work for everyone in the area. He also wanted to
destroy cargo cult, but he thought he must win the confidence
of its supporters first. As he himself graphically put it in private,
'You must not throw stones to kill a hen. You must come up
with food first and later kill the hen.' It was unfortunate for Job
and Pangu that this second aim, by its very nature, could not be
publicly announced, and that the first was widely misinterpreted
and misunderstood. To further his aims Job became a close
companion of the Kesup *lo bos*, a kinsman of his, attended meetings
of *lo bos* at Kesup, and encouraged correspondence and personal
contact between Pangu officials and the Regional candidate and
Yali himself. An important enabling factor in getting out the
cargo vote for Job was the absence of a candidate from the ranks
of the cultists themselves. Yali himself did not stand anywhere,
but he was widely reported to have endorsed three of his followers
in electorates where he had some support. But his nominee in
the Madang Open for some reason did not complete nomination
formalities, and so the Madang cargo cultists, in their own words,
were without a candidate who was truly their own. As one told
me: 'If Adei or Beig had stood, we wouldn't have had this
Pangu business'.

But apart from the specific events and personalities of 1972,
the ideological similarities between the cargo and Pangu messages
were also important for the alliance between them. As one cultist
explained, 'Pangu came. We went and saw that its policy was
like the Old Man [Yali's] talk.' The pre-existing polarization of
views also predisposed Christians to the views on self-government of Angmai and the United Party. This polarization also

affected the way in which people assessed rumours about the two parties' policies. Thus, when considering Pangu's policy on the role of whites after self-government, Christians could choose whether or not they believed its protestations of desire to co-operate with Europeans. In the event most Christians thought Pangu wanted to throw out whites. Madangs are used to thinking and acting in terms of the two opposing sides. It is an extremely difficult operation for anyone to try to bridge the gap between them. In the 1968 election Whitaker discovered this to his and Bato's cost, and in 1972 Job's friendship with the cultists lost him some, if not the majority of, Christian votes. One young educated Christian told me that he had wanted to join Pangu but had thought better of it. He said, 'Pangu is a real national party [*em i asples tru*]. But it is weak because of cargo cult.'

The internal organization of the Yali movement was significant for Pangu Pati in the 1972 elections. Through the network of *lo bos* and a hierarchy of officials somewhat expanded since 1969, information about policies and meetings was easily disseminated. At a meeting of *lo bos* at Kesup on 12 February, there were 17 men from 11 of the Madang villages plus 40 or so other village cult leaders. After it closed an announcement was made about the Pangu rally in town the next day. Cult and church organization also provided opportunities for interaction and discussion among members.

Thus, as could be expected from the data on the 1968 national elections, national political parties in Madang became enmeshed not in pragmatic but in ideological conflict. At least in the context of national elections, the parties have further institutional-ized the internal organization of each side and the relationship of opposition between them. However, elsewhere in Papua New Guinea, the same national parties appear to have become involved in what I have described for Madang as pragmatic conflict, the competition between traditional local groupings. Voutas (1972) states that in the Morobe District ethnic groups were the basis for recruitment to Pangu branches, and that there was 'little or no concept of divided opinion at the village level'. But although in Morobe ethnic groups were not divided between parties, these groups did constitute conflicting elements *within* the party at the level of the whole electorate. Thus there were several Pangu candidates in the Bulolo Open electorate, each endorsed by a different ethnic group. The absence of effective opposition to Pangu at the local level has left ethnic feeling free to assert itself in Morobe. Madang, on the other hand, while its villages and language groups are ideologically divided, has seen the development of a more genuine supra-village and supra-ethnic commitment to party interests.

Footnote, November 1973

In the latter half of 1972 and the early months of 1973 there appears to have been a major change in Yali's public position on the cargo cult aspects of his career and organization. He and fellow Sor villagers have issued a public statement dissociating his name from cargo cult. He himself wrote to me in September 1973: 'Some of the things you heard in Kauris were not mine, they were just lies. This work that they have said will cause something to come up without effort [cargo], this talk has been going on for a long time. It is the talk of the Madangs proper and it is not my talk.'

It does not seem to me that these statements invalidate earlier work done by Lawrence and myself. Indeed we have both recognised the way in which the cargo movement has had a momentum somewhat separate from that injected into it personally by Yali. Lawrence himself has been back to Madang during 1973 and feels that the change is due to certain new factors, namely a power struggle within the movement and pressures from outside (personal communication, August 1973).

Since I have not been in Madang since May 1972, I cannot say what have been the implications of these events for the Madang villages. To raise the matter at all must then seem tantalizing in the extreme to the majority of readers. However, this book may well be read by people within Papua New Guinea; it therefore seems to me to be fair to Yali to record what he clearly wishes to be known as his current thinking on an issue which is of such central importance in this book.

APPENDIX I

Methodological Data

SURVEY I. MARRIAGE AND FAMILY

This survey was an attempt to collect systematically from a number of different villages information on certain aspects of marriage and family. After a 100 per cent pilot survey in Kauris, an interview schedule was drawn up covering age, marital status, residence, parents' marriage(s), siblings, income, agriculture, own marriage(s), brideprice, children, adoptions involved in own marriage(s) and termination of marriage(s). The population from which my sample was drawn included men and women who had reached their 15th birthday on or before 30 September 1968. This age was selected because a pilot survey suggested that it was the earliest age of marriage, but since the survey proper revealed that a few women had married at 14 in the past, it may be that I misjudged the age-range needed. In line with the general argument of this book, and because of the need for reasonably accurate population lists, only land-owning males were included. Women who had never been married were included if their legal guardians were landowners and were listed as members of the villages of such men. Married women were included in their husbands' villages and widows and divorcees, who could be satisfactorily classified by neither of these methods, were recorded under their village of residence. Such a system was not intended as anything more than a convenient way of arranging the population in mutually exclusive and accessible categories for the purpose of sampling. Because of my indecision about the area of my study, I included in Survey I only 13 of the 17 villages, omitting Butelkud, Haidurem, Kesup and Mukuru. While this is undoubtedly unsatisfactory, I do not, on reflection, think that it biases my findings, since there are considerable similarities of social structure among all the villages discussed.

Population lists were drawn up by referring to Ambenob

Council's taxation and death registers, the Mabuso Electoral Roll, church records and village books. The lists thus compiled were then checked with senior clan members, and duplicated, foreign and deceased persons cut out. It was at this stage that comprehensive details on foreigners were recorded. However this by no means perfected the lists. Apart from undetected errors, a total of 25 persons were omitted from the final lists, 22 were included when they should not have been (including seven sample members and an eighth by replacement) and seven appeared twice. In relation to a total population of 1,259, these errors are not inconsiderable and may, in particular, have biased the sample against those (especially women) who for various reasons were less clearly attached to a particular village than the majority. The other main weakness in the population lists was that in practice I had to include those born between 30 September and the end of 1952 since official records rarely gave exact day and month of birth. Thus about one-quarter of those included in the population lists as 15-year-olds should not have been included. In addition, interviewing sometimes brought to light inaccuracies in the official records of age, which again affected the composition of the sample.

A total of 180 persons was selected randomly from the population, a sample of one in seven being drawn from the lists in such a way that each of the 13 villages was proportionately represented to the nearest seven members of its population. This was not done for comparative purposes but to ensure that small villages away from roads and amenities all had reasonable representation. While this survey yielded a random sample for the purposes of personal data (age, own adoption etc.), it could not do the same for marriages and adoptions involving ego's children. In those cases my analysis does not rest on a random sample of marriages and adoptions occurring in a certain area in a given period of time, but on those in which a random sample of individuals was involved. (Duplicated cases were counted only once.)

As I proceeded several weaknesses in the questions and interviewing procedure became apparent. For instance I was asking for too much detail about events which for some had happened half a lifetime ago. Other questions were not flexible enough or, if they were, the answers did not lend themselves to quantification.

I had chosen to conduct interviews with other relatives present in the hope that their recollections would increase the accuracy with which distant events were recalled. I underestimated informants' sensitivity on some of the topics. Had I interviewed each sample member privately on such subjects as divorce, I might well have received different answers. The survey probably attempted to cover too many subjects and therefore covered few really well, the most valuable data being on age, marriage and adoption directions, age at and reason for adoption, fertility and sequence of marriage arrangements, and the weakest areas being brideprice and divorce.

Non-response was low, since for absent sample members I collected data from relatives and supplemented this in some cases with correspondence with the person himself. As a result there were only 2 cases out of 180 in which I could obtain no information whatsoever. In both these cases relatives of absent persons would not cooperate. Data from Surveys I and II were analysed with the help of the Computer Services Unit of the London School of Economics.

SURVEY II. CHRISTIANS AND CULTISTS

This survey was designed to relate certain variables to participation in Yali's movement and church activities. Questions were asked about cult and church affiliation, age, education, employment history, income, assets, participation in earlier cults, voting in elections and the position of various relatives on the Yali issue. It is not to my credit that no pilot survey was done for the interview schedule. As a result I chose to change it about half-way through and conducted 45 of the 94 interviews with an improved version. In retrospect I realize that there was no value in the change, since the number of cases for which I had the additional information was so small.

The main weakness of Survey II was the small size of the sample. To save time I decided to use the Survey I sample plus additional members from Butelkud, Haidurem, Kesup and Mukuru selected in the same way. I was also of the opinion that it would not be particularly useful to interview women, since the major determinant of their overt ideological allegiance appeared to be that of their father or husband (see Chapter 6). I therefore had a sample of roughly one in 14 and a total of 111 men. This was further reduced by a higher non-response rate than that for Survey I, caused by the necessity to conduct all interviews in person and in private. Out of the total sample, 12 informants were absent, 2 were dead before I could interview them, and 3 (all cargo cultists) refused to cooperate. With only 94 cases for analysis and three distinct groups within the sample (Christians, cultists and 'neithers'), few of my findings were significant at the 5 per cent level.

A further question-mark hangs over the honesty with which informants answered my questions on these very sensitive topics. The questions were framed particularly to cover only public or semi-public actions, such as payment of taxes to Yali, and not to probe into any private reservations that a man might have had about his public position. The most likely areas for inaccurate responses were questions about personal financial assets and participation in previous cults.

SURVEY III.   MARRIAGES,   RESIDENCE,   CLANS   AND AFFILIATION

This survey was designed to establish the original village and clan of women currently married to land-owning males in the 17 villages, the place of residence of these males, their clan membership and their publicly stated position on Yali and Christianity. It covered all 817 men in the villages under study.

Once again I used the population lists drawn up for Surveys I and II. In fact the establishment of clan membership had been one of the essential steps in drawing up these lists in the first place. Thus Survey III was made in the course of preparation for Surveys I and II, but it is included separately here because its reliability depends on slightly different factors. Since no sampling was involved, amendments to the lists on which the results of Survey III are based were made up to the end of the fieldwork period. Hence they contain no errors in them of which I am aware, though I am sure there are at least a few which I do not know about.

Clearly it was both impracticable and unnecessary to interview all 817 men personally. Therefore, as already indicated, I sat down and went through my lists with senior members of each clan. Where doubt was expressed, particularly on the exact origin of wives or where an absent member lived, others were consulted. The only question over which some problem might have arisen is that about attitudes to Yali and Christianity. But political allegiance is a matter of public statements which are generally known. I recall that when I first began talking to Kauris people about cargo cult, I was inundated with repetitions of identical lists of allegiances in the village, lists which I have since had no cause to amend and which people were most anxious that I got straight. I feel fairly confident, therefore, that, while my quantitative data, both in this survey and Survey II, reflect no subtle shades of ideological difference, they nevertheless adequately record the public allegiances the surveys were intended to investigate.

SURVEY IV. VILLAGE TERRITORY AND CULT PARTICIPATION

In preparation for my analysis of inter-village marriages (see Appendix II) and as general background for topics such as land disputes, I felt that I needed to know which villages had territory adjacent to those under study. I also wanted to collect from each of the 17 villages information on their past participation in cargo cults and the means by which each cult was introduced into the village. These questions related to the village as a whole and were, therefore, asked only of two or three informants in each village. For this reason the collection of this material is given a separate number, although in practice the survey was conducted simultaneously with parts of Surveys I to III. The information solicited on land boundaries was almost entirely an objective matter, though the *location* of these boundaries might have been a less neutral topic. My questions on cargo cults received a somewhat more subjective response. Often informants said their village had not really taken part in X cult, they had just 'tried it out', or had built a house 'in case anything came of it'. It was impossible to establish what their attitudes had been at the time of the events. My suspicion was that in many cases the informants had either not taken part themselves or were ashamed of the failure of their efforts and were rewriting their own history. So I rephrased my questions to establish if *any* member of their villages had done anything in connection with the cult in question. Frequently this would produce an account of some activities, embellished with the usual disclaimers. I would then press on to ask how this person, and through him other members of the village, became involved in the first place. Over certain cults people were quite open. Nobody seemed to be ashamed of Letub, so that my material on that cult is pretty full. But people were much more reluctant to admit involvement in Owro's cult. I feel, therefore, that despite cross-checking with informants elsewhere, my final conclusions may somewhat underestimate the incidence of the cults in different villages.

Inter-village Marriages

This analysis was designed to test the significance and relative significance of three variables for the incidence of marriages between villages. The variables are language, distance between villages and whether or not villages have adjacent territory. This last was included because it seemed possible that a short distance between villages might be less significant when there was an intervening village. The results were intended to be related later to leadership patterns and the extent of kinship networks.

The raw data came from Survey III, and are set out in Table 22. This covers all current marriages in the 17 villages. These were classified, as shown in Table 23, according to the three selected variables. Information on languages came from Z'graggen (1969). Distances between villages were determined from official maps (D.L.S.M., Fourmil and Milinch Series 1965), although I amended village sites to correspond with the current position of the largest hamlet in each village. Survey IV had ascertained which villages had adjacent territory. All wives come from within Madang District, except those in the column headed 'O.D.', Out of District. Two detailed points should be noted. The four wives in Opi who come from adjacent villages in a different language group all come from Gal. Two of the Gal women married into the Areh section of the administrative unit of Opi. Areh traditionally spoke the Gal language. Two married into Opi proper, i.e. Isebe-speaking Opi. All four are included here because today both Areh and Opi commonly speak Isebe. Of the Urugan wives who come from adjacent villages, one of the seven from within the language group and all three from within the language family come from villages more than three and less than six miles away. All other cases of adjacent villages are within three miles.

To test the significance of the selected variables it was necessary to be able to compare actual marriages with those that would

Table 22. Origin of wives in current marriages in the 17 villages

Wives in \ from	BAR	BUT	FOR	HAI	KAM	KAU	KES	KOR	MIR	MIS	MUK	NOB	OPI	PAN	SIL	URU	YAH
Barahaim	17	—	—	—	—	—	—	9	3	—	—	—	—	1	—	3	—
Butelkud	—	9	—	—	1	—	—	2	—	—	—	—	—	—	—	—	—
Foran	—	—	4	8	—	1	—	—	—	—	—	—	—	—	—	—	—
Haidurem	—	1	—	—	—	—	—	—	—	—	3	1	—	—	—	—	—
Kamba	—	—	—	—	51	6	—	—	—	—	—	3	—	—	3	—	—
Kauris	—	—	1	—	3	14	—	2	—	1	1	1	—	2	4	—	—
Kesup	—	—	—	—	—	1	4	16	1	—	—	—	—	—	—	—	—
Korog	8	2	1	—	—	1	1	3	1	1	—	—	6	1	1	2	1
Mirkuk	—	—	1	—	—	1	2	—	11	—	—	—	1	2	—	1	—
Mis	—	—	—	—	2	—	—	—	—	11	—	2	—	2	1	—	—
Mukuru	—	—	1	5	—	—	—	—	—	—	9	—	—	—	—	—	—
Nobanob	—	—	—	4	—	—	—	—	—	2	2	60	—	—	2	—	—
Opi	1	—	—	—	—	—	—	—	—	—	—	—	—	—	—	1	—
Panim	2	—	2	—	2	2	—	2	2	1	—	—	—	7	1	—	—
Silabob	—	1	2	—	—	3	—	3	—	—	—	—	—	1	5	—	—
Urugan	2	—	—	—	—	—	—	—	—	—	—	—	—	—	—	6	—
Yahil	—	—	—	—	—	—	—	—	4	—	—	—	—	—	—	—	—
Other in Madang District																	
Abar	—	—	1	—	—	—	—	—	—	—	—	—	—	—	—	—	—
Aguru	—	—	—	—	—	—	1	—	—	—	—	—	—	—	—	—	—
Aijap	—	—	1	—	—	—	—	—	—	—	—	—	—	—	—	—	—
Arar	1	—	—	—	1	—	—	—	—	—	—	—	—	—	—	—	—

Table 22 (cont.)

Wives in	BAR	BUT	FOR	HAI	KAM	KAU	KES	KOR	MIR	MIS	MUK	NOB	OPI	PAN	SIL	URU	YAH
Bagesin area			1														
Baipa				2													
Banup							1		1								
Bemahal													1			1	
Birimai																1	
Bogia area																	
Bunabun area												1					
Bundi area					1												
Dolonu	2			1												2	
Efu	1							1									
Gal		1											4				
Garigut				1													
Guhup		2		1													
Gumalu											1						
Haiya									1								
Hapurpi											1						1
Hilu							2										
Karkar Is.												1		2			
Kosilanta area											1						
Laigna											1						
Mabanob																	
Mainan				1				1									
Manah		1														1	
Matepi						1											

Table 22 (cont.)

Wives in	BAR	BUT	FOR	HAI	KAM	KAU	KES	KOR	MIR	MIS	MUK	NOB	OPI	PAN	SIL	URU	YAH
Meginam	—	—	—	—	—	—	—	—	1	—	—	—	—	—	—	—	—
Mirhanak	—	—	—	—	—	—	—	—	—	—	—	—	—	—	—	—	1
Moilsehu	—	—	—	—	—	—	1	—	—	—	—	—	—	—	—	1	—
Nake	—	1	—	—	—	—	—	—	—	—	—	—	—	—	—	—	—
Ohu	2	—	—	—	—	—	2	—	—	—	—	—	—	—	—	—	—
Ord	—	—	—	—	—	—	1	—	—	—	—	—	—	—	—	—	—
Rai Coast area	—	—	—	—	—	—	—	—	—	—	—	—	—	—	—	—	—
Sa	1	—	—	—	—	—	—	—	—	—	—	—	—	—	—	1	—
Saluku	—	—	—	—	—	—	—	—	—	1	—	—	—	1	—	1	—
Senpi	—	—	1	—	—	—	—	—	—	—	—	—	—	—	—	—	—
Sohia	—	—	2	—	—	—	—	—	—	—	—	—	—	—	—	—	—
Sua	—	—	—	—	—	—	—	—	—	—	—	—	—	—	—	—	—
Wama	—	—	—	—	—	—	1	—	—	—	—	—	—	—	—	—	—
Wangar	—	—	—	—	—	—	4	—	—	—	1	—	—	—	—	—	2
Yelso	—	—	—	—	—	—	—	—	—	—	—	—	—	—	—	—	—
Yoidik	—	—	—	—	—	—	—	—	—	1	—	—	—	—	—	—	—
Outside Madang District	5	1	2	—	1	3	2	4	3	6	—	—	—	2	—	1	—
Total	41	20	20	24	62	33	22	43	28	24	20	69	12	21	16	22	5

Table 23. Sources of wives outside own village classified according to three selected variables

Language Location (in miles)	Own				Same family different language					Different language family						Not known		All
	Adj	Non-Adj <3	<6	<9	Adj	Non-Adj <3	<6	<9	9+	Adj	Non-Adj <3	<6	<9	9+	O.D.	Adj Non-Adj	D.K.	
Barahaim	13	—	—	—	—	—	6	—	—	—	—	—	—	—	5	—	—	24
Butelkud	2	—	—	—	1	—	4	—	—	—	2	—	—	—	1	—	1	11
Foran	3	—	1	—	—	—	1	—	1	2	1	3	—	1	2	—	1	16
Haidurem	10	1	1	—	—	—	—	—	—	—	—	1	—	1	1	1	—	16
Kamba	3	—	—	—	—	—	—	1	—	—	—	—	—	4	3	—	—	11
Kauris	9	—	2	—	—	2	—	1	—	—	—	2	—	—	2	—	—	19
Kesup	6	1	—	—	—	—	4	—	—	—	—	—	—	1	4	—	2	18
Korog	14	3	—	—	—	—	1	—	—	2	2	2	—	—	3	—	—	27
Mirkuk	2	1	—	—	4	—	2	1	—	—	—	—	—	—	6	—	1	17
Mis	1	2	1	—	2	—	1	—	2	—	1	2	1	—	—	—	—	13
Mukuru	4	2	2	—	—	—	—	—	—	—	1	—	—	1	—	—	1	11
Nobanob	1	2	—	—	5	1	—	—	—	—	—	—	—	—	—	—	—	9
Opi	6	1	—	—	—	—	—	—	—	4	—	1	—	—	—	—	—	12
Panim	4	—	—	—	—	—	3	—	—	3	1	1	—	—	2	—	—	14
Silabob	8	—	—	—	2	—	—	—	—	—	1	—	—	—	—	—	—	11
Urugan	7	—	—	—	3	—	3	—	—	—	—	—	—	1	1	1	—	16
Yahil	3	2	—	—	—	—	—	—	—	—	—	—	—	—	—	—	—	5
	96	13	11	1	20	3	25	3	3	12	7	7	1	11	30	1	6	250

have taken place if the variables were not significant. I had to set up another table on the hypothesis of a random distribution of marriages between categories. I therefore compiled Table 24, which indicates what would have happened if one wife came from every village in every category. For this purpose I described circles with radii of three, six and nine miles for each of the 17 villages. Using the linguistic and geographical data already mentioned I was then able to see how many villages fell into each category for each of the 17 under study. The choice of distances was arbitrary, being designed only to produce an evenly spaced sequence. It is obvious that the longer the distance the more villages will fall into each category. Therefore it appeared necessary to limit the investigation to a reasonably short distance. This procedure was practically expedient, and can also be justified on other grounds. Only 44 of the 243 marriages for which all information is available were with villages more than nine miles away; and 30 of these were outside the District. In this latter category, the small number of marriages in relation to the vast number of villages in the whole of Papua New Guinea (or even neighbouring districts) makes comparison meaningless as well as impracticable. Moreover, such marriages do not appear to be important for Madang politics. The remaining 14 marriages were mainly with areas within the District but so far away as again to be irrelevant to village politics. In fact in seven cases the names of the villages were unknown to informants; they referred simply to the 'Rai Coast' or 'Bunabun' for example. Only 2 of the 14 (Abar and Efu) were within Ambenob Council area. It therefore appeared both practical and reasonable to limit my analysis to a distance of nine miles, while recognizing the existence of the 44 marriages beyond that limit. (The position of one village which is starred in Table 24 was assumed because it was neither entered on the official maps nor actually visited by me.)

A comparison of the totals for Tables 23 and 24 shows clearly that, in terms of the selected variables, the distribution of marriages is far from random. In order to rank the three variables in order of importance Table 25 was compiled. This relates the observed to the expected frequency in each category. A ratio was calculated by dividing the first by the second. However the total figures are more valuable than the internal cell figures because for the

Language Location (in miles)	Own					Same family different language					Different language family				
	Adj		Non-Adj			Adj		Non-Adj			Adj		Non-Adj		
	<3	<6	<3	<6	<9	<3	<6	<3	<6	<9	<3	<6	<3	<6	<9
Barahaim	5	—	—	—	—	1	—	1	35	—	—	—	2	6	21
Butelkud	4	—	—	8	6	—	—	—	12	11	—	—	2	5	26
Foran	2	—	—	8	2	—	1	—	2	8	3	—	5	23	16
Haidurem	4	—	4	8	2	2	1	—	8	16	—	—	1	6	8
Kamba	2	—	—	2	—	—	—	1	11	14	2	—	—	12	36
Kauris	2	—	—	2	—	—	—	—	10	14	2	—	3	14	32
Kesup	3	—	4	17	1	—	—	—	4	6	2	—	1	8	5
Korog	4	—	1	—	—	2	—	—	26	12	2	—	2	16	23
Mirkuk	1	—	2	2	—	1	3	2	28	3	—	—	3	8	22
Mis	2	1	2	2	—	—	—	—	2	13	2	—	1	16	20
Mukuru	4	—	3	8	2	3	—	—	9	22	—	—	—	2	12
Nobanob	1	—	—	10	4	—	—	1	1	10	2	—	—	12	19
Opi	2	—	1	2	—	1	—	—	15	23	3	1	2	14	24
Panim	3	—	—	2	—	1	—	1	27	9	1	—	—	10	21
Silabob	4	—	—	—	—	—	—	—	4	16	3	—	4	24	23
Urugan	3	1	—	1	—	2	3	1	22	12	1*	1	—	17	28
Yahil	2	—	13	10	—	—	—	1	10	5	—	—	2	9	23
Language totals	48	2	28	76	15	13	8	8	226	194	23	2	28	202	359
	169					449					614				
Grand total	1,232														

latter the numbers in the original tables are sometimes very small. It appears that the highest rate (1·28) is for villages with adjacent territory, the second highest (0·993) for villages within three miles of each other and the third (0·716) for villages speaking the same language. The greatest likelihood of marriage (a rate of 1·98) occurs at the intersection of these three categories.

Table 25. Comparison of Tables 23 and 24 giving an observed rate of marriage for an average village in each category

Language		Own	Same family, different language	Different language family	All
Location:					
Adjacent:	<3	1·98	1·31	0·522	1·48
	<6	0·5	0·375	—	0·333
Non-adjacent:	<3	0·464	0·375	0·25	0·359
	<6	0·145	0·11	0·0346	0·0852
	<9	0·0667	0·0155	0·00278	0·0088
Totals	<3	1·42	0·952	0·372	0·993
	<6	0·154	0·019	0·00336	0·0911
	<9	0·0667	0·0155	0·00279	0·0088
Total adjacent		1·92	0·952	0·479	1·28
Total non-adjacent		0·21	0·0725	0·0253	0·0624
Grand total		0·716	0·114	0·044	

LIST OF WORKS CITED

ABAL, T. 1972. 'United Party Policy Statement', in *House of Assembly Elections 1972. What do Political Parties want for Papua New Guinea?* (J. A. Chan, T. Abal and M. T. Somare), Port Moresby.

The Australian, 20 December 1968, Sydney.

BAILEY, F. G., 1969. *Stratagems and Spoils*, Oxford.

BOTTOMORE, T. B., 1965. *Classes in Modern Society*, London.

COMMONWEALTH OF AUSTRALIA, 1967/68. *Territory of New Guinea Report*, Canberra.

CROCOMBE, R., 1968. 'Local Government in New Guinea: an Example of Conflict between Policy and Practice', *Journal of Pacific History*, 3.

DOUGLAS, M., 1970. *Natural Symbols*, London.

EVANGELICAL LUTHERAN CONGREGATION OF NEW GUINEA, 1958. Annual Report for Amele Circuit.

FAIRBAIRN, I. J. *et al.*, 1969. 'NAMASU: New Guinea's Largest Indigenous Owned Company', *New Guinea Research Bulletin*, 28.

FISCHER, D., 1955. *Unter Südsee-Insularnern. Das Leben des Forschers Mikloucho-Maclay*, Leipzig.

FLIERL, J., 1931. *Forty-five Years in New Guinea*, Columbus.

FOSTER, G. M., 1967. 'What is a peasant?', in *Peasant Society. A Reader* (J. M. Potter *et al.*), Boston.

GLUCKMAN, M., 1956. *Custom and Conflict in Africa*, Oxford.

HARDING, T. G., 1967. *Voyagers of the Vitiaz Strait*, Seattle and London.

HARDING, T. G. and LAWRENCE, P., 1971. 'Cash Crops or Cargo?', in *The Politics of Dependence* (A. L. Epstein, R. S. Parker and M. Reay, eds.), Canberra.

HAU'OFA, E., 1971. 'Mekeo Chieftainship', *Journal of the Polynesian Society*, 80, no. 2.

HOGBIN, H. I. and WEDGWOOD, C., 1953. 'Local Grouping in Melanesia', *Oceania*, XXII, no. 4.

HOGG, L. and ROBERTSON, S., 1971. 'The Madang Earthquake: Six Weeks After', *Oceania*, XLI, no. 4.

HUGHES, C. A., 1965. 'Development of the Legislature: Preparing for the House of Assembly', in *The Papua-New Guinea Elections, 1964* (D. G. Bettison *et al.*), Canberra.

HUGHES, C. A. and VAN DER VEUR, P. W., 1965. 'The Elections: an Overview', in *The Papua-New Guinea Elections, 1964* (D. G. Bettison *et al.*), Canberra.

HUGHES, D. T., 1969. 'Democracy in a Traditional Society: Two Hypotheses on Role', *American Anthropologist*, 71, no. 1.

IMPERIAL GERMAN GOVERNMENT, 1906. *Deutsches Koloniablatt: Amtsblatt für die Schutzgebiete des Deutschen Reiches* (edited in the Colonial Department of the Foreign Office), XVII.

IMPERIAL GERMAN GOVERNMENT, 1911. *Amtsblatt für das Schutzgebiet Deutsch-Neu Guinea*, III.

INSELMANN, R., 1944. Letub, the Cult of the Secrets of Wealth, M.A. thesis submitted to the faculty of the Kennedy School of Missions, Hartford Seminary Foundation.

LAWRENCE, P., 1964. *Road Belong Cargo*, Manchester.

—, No date. Unpublished field notes on the 1968 elections.

—, 1970. 'The Widening Political Arena in the Southern Madang District', in *The Politics of Melanesia* (M. Ward, ed.), Canberra and Port Moresby.

LEYS, C., 1967. *Politicians and Policies*, Nairobi.

LUTHERAN MISSION, MADANG, 1969. School registers at Baitabag, Lutheran Day and Nobanob Primary 'T' Schools.

MADANG WORKERS' ASSOCIATION. Register of Members.

MALINOWSKI, B., 1922. *Argonauts of the Western Pacific*, London.

MEISER, L., 1955. 'The "Platform" Phenomenon along the Northern Coast of New Guinea', *Anthropos*, 50.

MORAUTA, L., 1972a. Beyond the village: a study of contemporary politics in the hinterland of Madang, New Guinea, Ph.D. thesis, University of London.

—, 1972b. 'The Politics of Cargo Cults in the Madang Area', *Man*, 7, no. 3.

—, (in press a). 'Traditional Polity in Madang', *Oceania*.

—, (in press b). 'National Parties and Local-level Politics: a View from Madang', in a volume on the 1972 national elections (D. Stone, ed.), Port Moresby.

PAPUA NEW GUINEA, 1968a. *Report of the Chief Electoral Officer on the House of Assembly Elections 1968*, Port Moresby.

—, 1968b. *Village Directory*, Port Moresby.

—, 1963–7, *Local Government Ordinance*, Port Moresby.

—, *Department of the Administrator, Bureau of Statistics*. Population Census – July 1971. Preliminary Bulletin No. 1. Urban Centres, mimeographed.

—, *Department of the Administrator, Division of District Administration* (formerly (a) Department of District Services and (b) Department of District Administration).

Ambenob Local Government Council (unpublished records, council head-quarters, Danben, near Madang).

Election files

Minutes of Executive and Finance Committee meetings

Minutes of General Meetings

Village census sheets

Ward voting registers

Annual Reports, Madang District. Archives, Port Moresby.

Census and Statistic Madang District. File 14-2-7. Records Section, Port Moresby.

Council Elections. File 1-4. Regional Local Government Office, Madang.

District Advisory Council. File 1-14-4. District Office, Madang.

District Councils Conference, Madang District. Duplicated Agenda.

Local Government Councils in New Guinea. File 42-4-2. District Office, Madang and D.D.A., Port Moresby.

Patrol Reports, Madang District. D.D.A., Port Moresby.

Quarterly Reports, Madang District. File 29-10-34. Archives, Port Moresby.

Silabob Village Book, held by council *komiti*, Silabob Village.

Special Report of A.D.O. Keenan, 21 January 1951. Archives, Port Moresby.

—, *Department of Agriculture, Stock and Fisheries.*

File 23-3-A(2). D.A.S.F. Office, Madang.

File 23-3-1(2). D.A.S.F. Office, Madang.

File 'Councillor Kaut. Agricultural Committee'. Held by Kaut Malok of Kauris in 1968.

Production Madang Central, 1967–68. File 38-2-A(1). D.A.S.F. Office, Madang.

Project Areas 6 and 7 (files on individual cocoa and coconut holdings). D.A.S.F. Office, Madang.

Registers of Members, Bel Society, Pau Society and Madang Cocoa Co-operative. D.A.S.F. Office, Madang.

—, *Department of Education*, 1969. School registers at Barahaim, Gum, Kamba, Kusbau and Sagalau Primary 'T' Schools.

—, *Department of Lands, Surveys and Mines.*

Fourmil and Milinch Series (1965):

  Milinch of Kranket N.E.

  Milinch of Kranket N.W.

  Milinch of Kranket S.E.

  Milinch of Kranket S.W. D.L.S.M., Port Moresby.

Madang 10 chain sheet (1971). D.L.S.M., Port Moresby.

Minutes of the Territory Lands Board. D.L.S.M., Port Moresby.

—, *Department of Social Development and Home Affairs.* Tally sheets used in counting votes in Madang Open electorate, 1972. District Office, Madang.

—, *Land Titles Commission.* Minutes of the Avisan Adjudication Area, Madang 14. File 19-14. L.T.C. Office, Madang.

Papua New Guinea Post-Courier, 17 February 1972, Port Moresby.

PARKER, R. S., 1966. 'The Advance to Responsible Government', in *New Guinea on the Threshold* (E. K. Fisk, ed.), Canberra.

RADCLIFFE-BROWN, A. R. and FORDE, D., 1950. *African Systems of Kinship and Marriage*, London.

REAY, M., 1970. 'Roads and Bridges between Three Levels of Politics', in *The Politics of Melanesia* (M. Ward, ed.), Canberra and Port Moresby.

ROWLEY, C. D., 1954. 'Native Officials and Magistrates of German New Guinea', 1897–1921, *South Pacific*, 7, no. 7.

RYAN, D., 1969. 'Christianity, Cargo Cults and Politics among the Toaripi of Papua', *Oceania*, XL, no. 2.

SAHLINS, M., 1966. 'Poor Man, Rich Man, Big-Man, Chief: Political Types in Melanesia and Polynesia', in *Readings in Australian and Pacific Anthropology* (I. Hogbin and L. R. Hiatt, eds.), Melbourne.

SCHWARTZ, T., 1962. 'The Paliau Movement in the Admiralty Islands, 1946–54', *Anthropological Papers of the American Museum of Natural History*, 49, part 2.

SELIGMAN, C. G., 1910. *The Melanesians of British New Guinea*, Cambridge.

SEVENTH DAY ADVENTIST MISSION, 1969. School register at Panim Primary 'T' School.

SOMARE, M. T., 1972. 'Pangu Pati Policy Statement', in *House of Assembly Elections 1972. What do Political Parties Want for Papua New Guinea?* (J. A. Chan, T. Abal and M. T. Somare), Port Moresby.

STEVENSON, M., 1968. A Trade Union in New Guinea, *Oceania*, XXXIX, no. 2.

STRATHERN, A., 1970. '*Kiap*, Councillor and Big Man: Role-contrasts in Mount Hagen', in *The Politics of Melanesia* (M. Ward, ed.), Canberra and Port Moresby.

TUSBAB HIGH SCHOOL, 1968. Urban Survey of Madang, carried out by Form IV students in November 1968, duplicated.

VOUTAS, A., 1972. The Growth of Pangu Pati in the Morobe District, unpublished paper given at a University of Papua and New Guinea extension lecture on 24 April 1972.

WILLIAMS, F. E., 1928. *Orokaiva Magic*, London.

—, 1936. *Papuans of the Trans-Fly*, Oxford.

WOLFERS, E., 1967. 'The Political Parties', *New Guinea*, 2, no. 3.

—, 1968/69. 'The Elections II', *New Guinea*, 3, no. 4.

WORSLEY, P. L., 1957. *The Trumpet Shall Sound*, London.

YOUNG, M. W., 1971. *Fighting with Food*, Cambridge.

Z'GRAGGEN, J. A., 1969. Classificatory and Typological Studies in Languages of the Western Madang District, New Guinea, Ph.D. thesis, Australian National University.

INDEX

Italic figures indicate principal reference

h